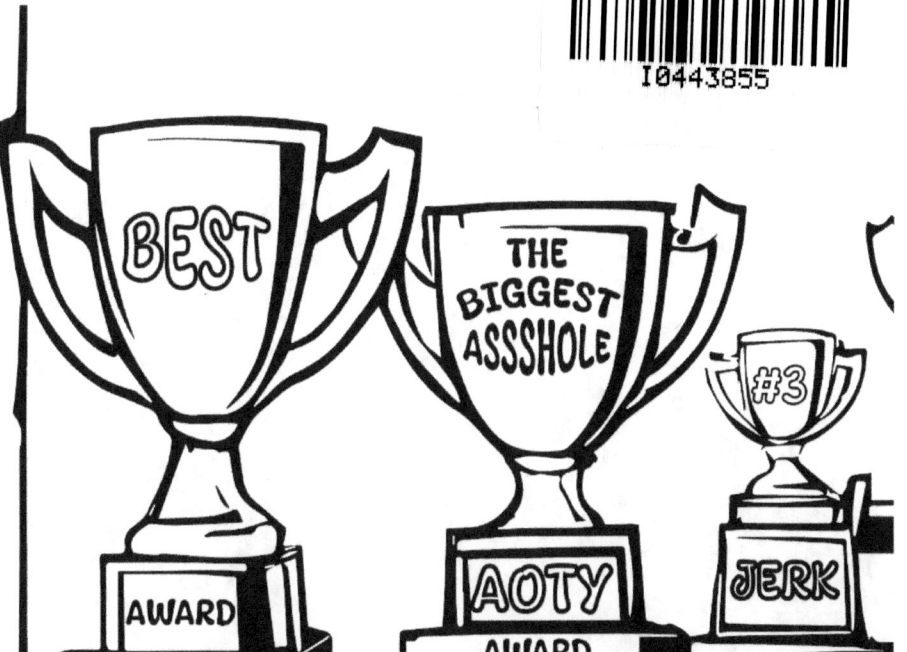

Prepare yourself for a wild ride! "Asshole of the Year" is not your grandma's coloring book. This hilarious and irreverent collection of swear words and cheeky phrases is intended for mature audiences with a wicked sense of humor. If colorful language offends you, it's best to turn back now, like RIGHT FUCKING NOW.

For everyone else, buckle the FUCK up! This book might cause uncontrollable laughter, a sudden urge to vent your frustrations creatively, and a newfound appreciation for artistic profanity. Side effects may include snorting, giggling, and an overwhelming sense of relief as you color away your stress.

No part of this publication may be reproduced, distributed, or transmitted in any form or by any means, including photocopying, recording, or other electronic or mechanical methods, without the prior written permission of the publisher, except in the case of brief quotations embodied in critical reviews and certain other noncommercial uses permitted by copyright law.

Copyright © 2024 by Grammwerks Media and Jay Mitchell. All rights reserved.

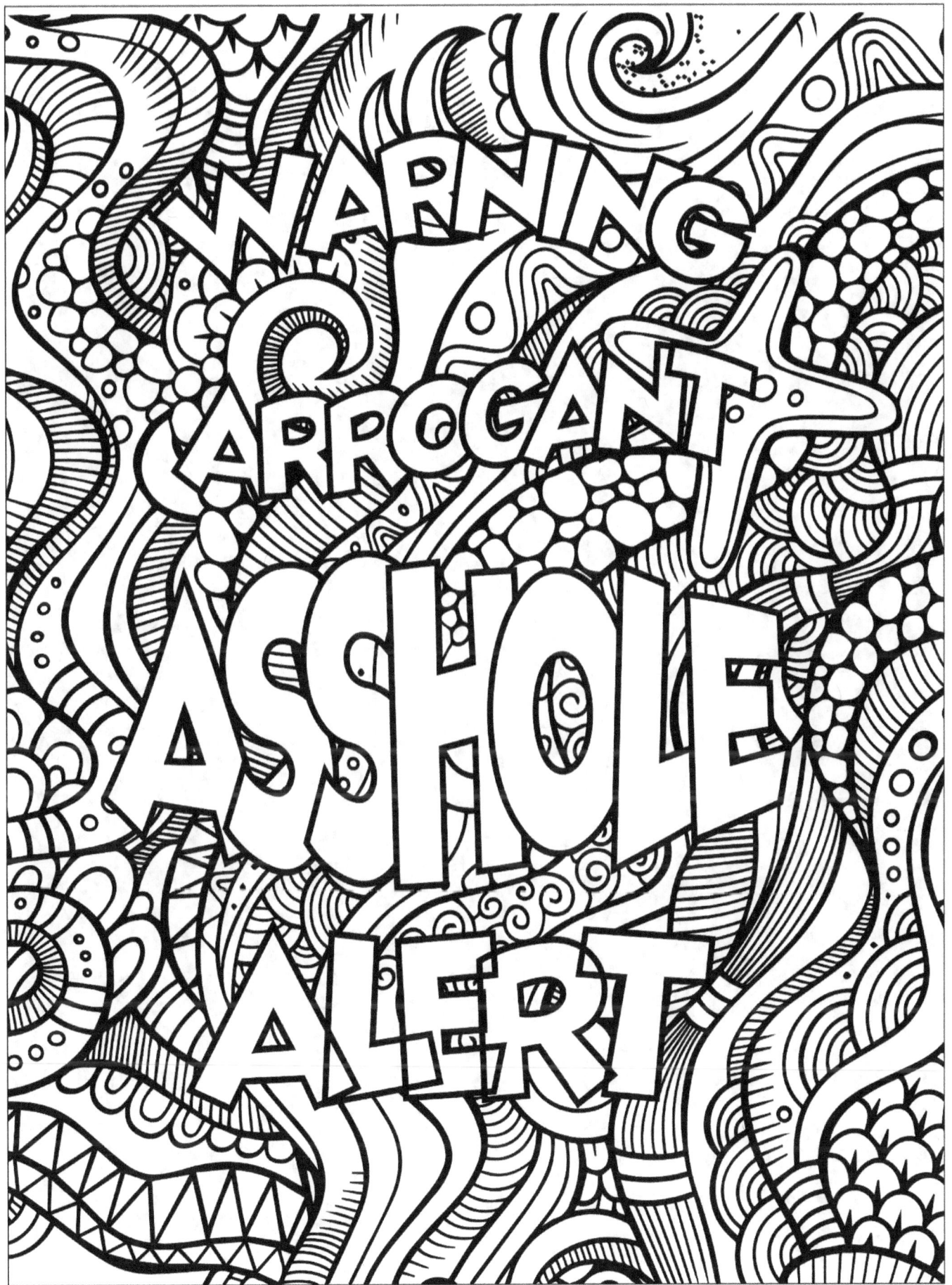

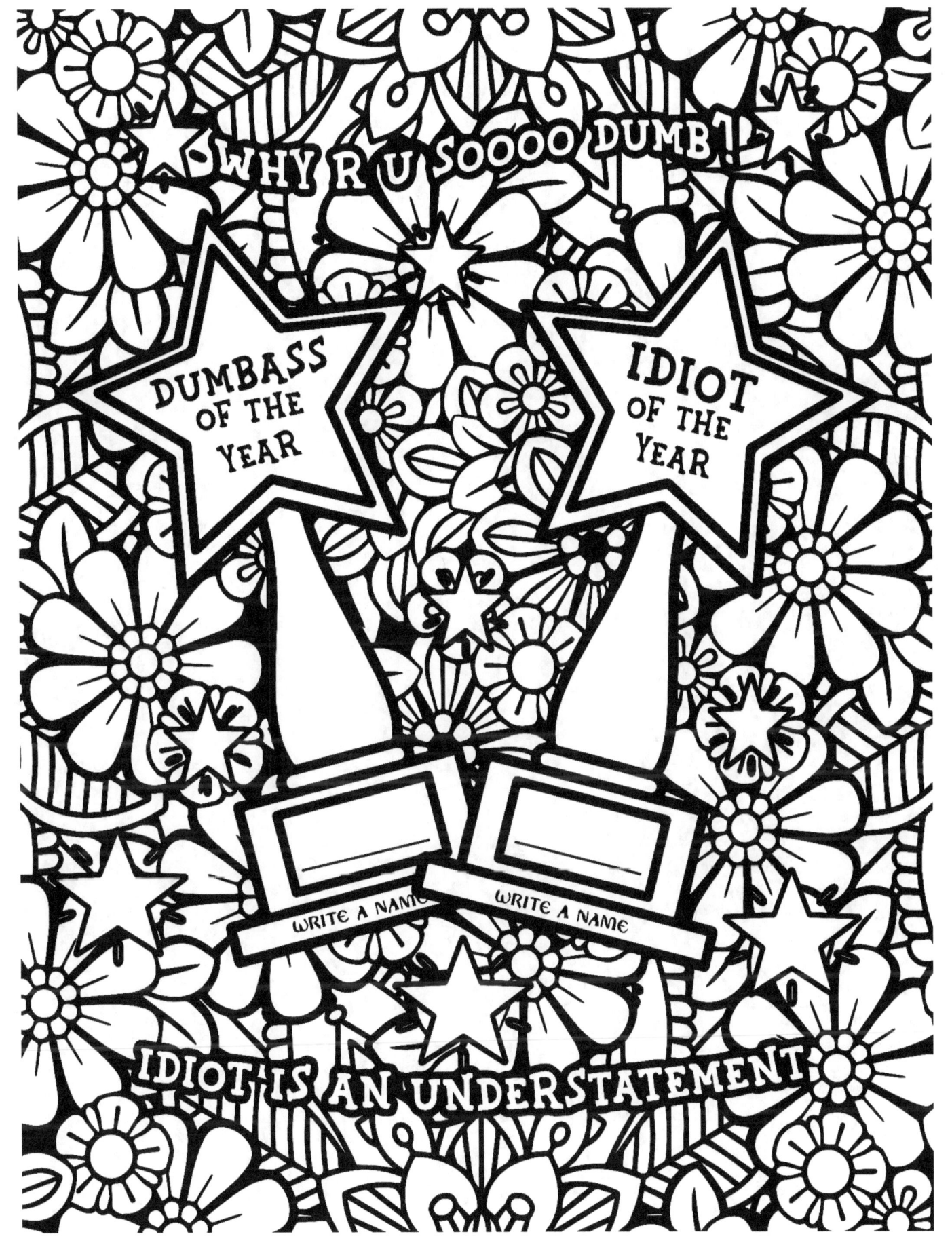

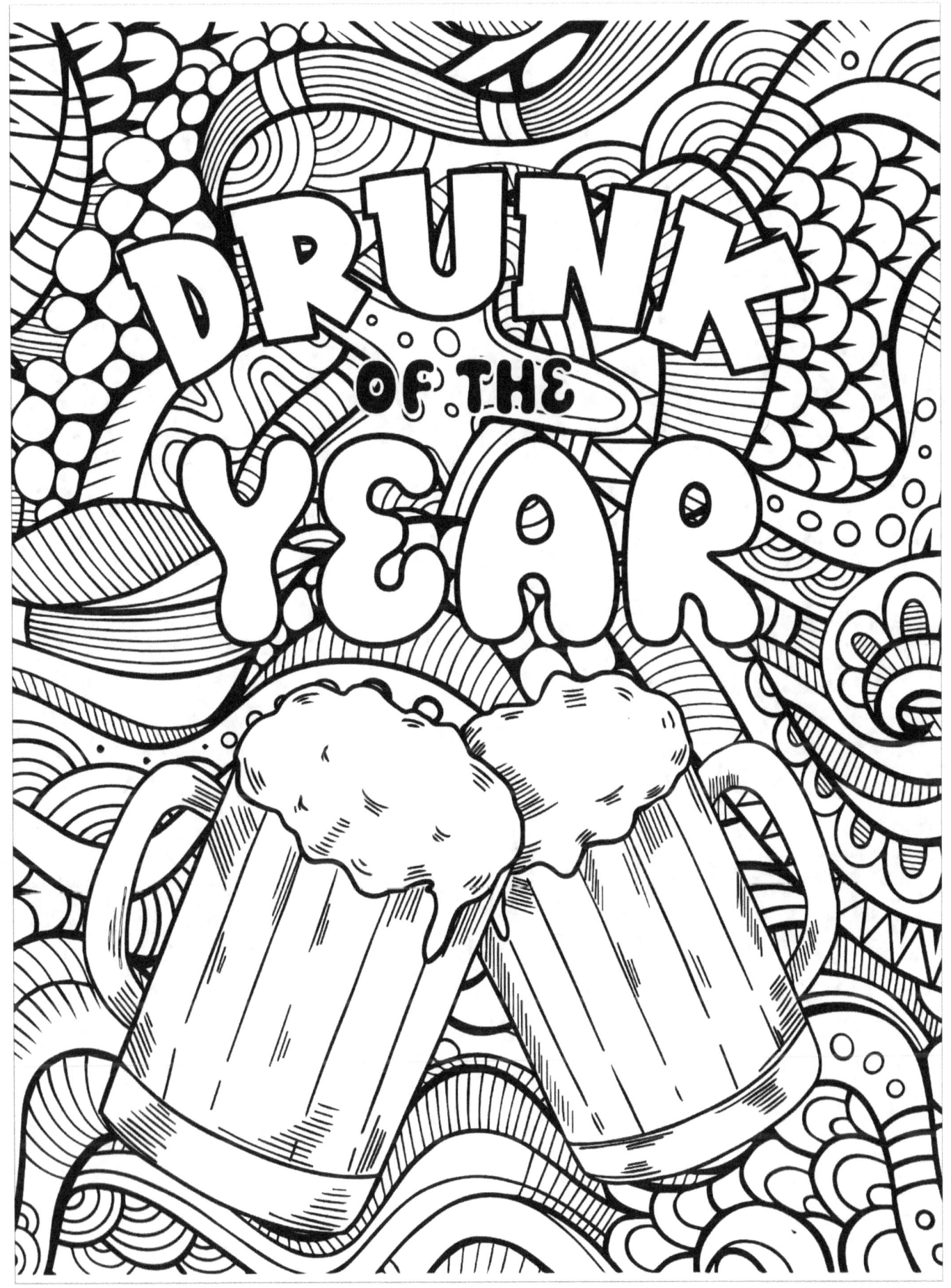

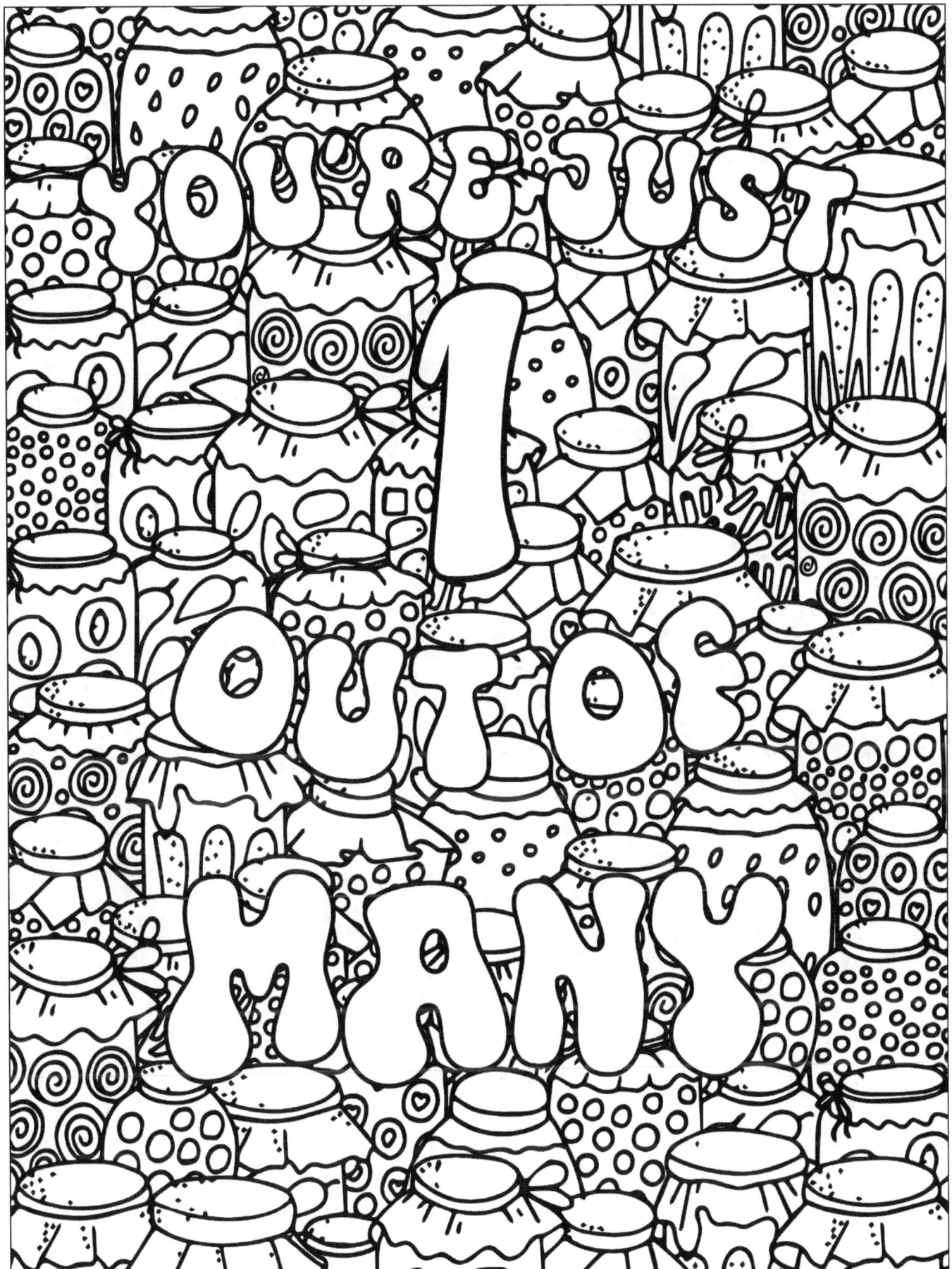

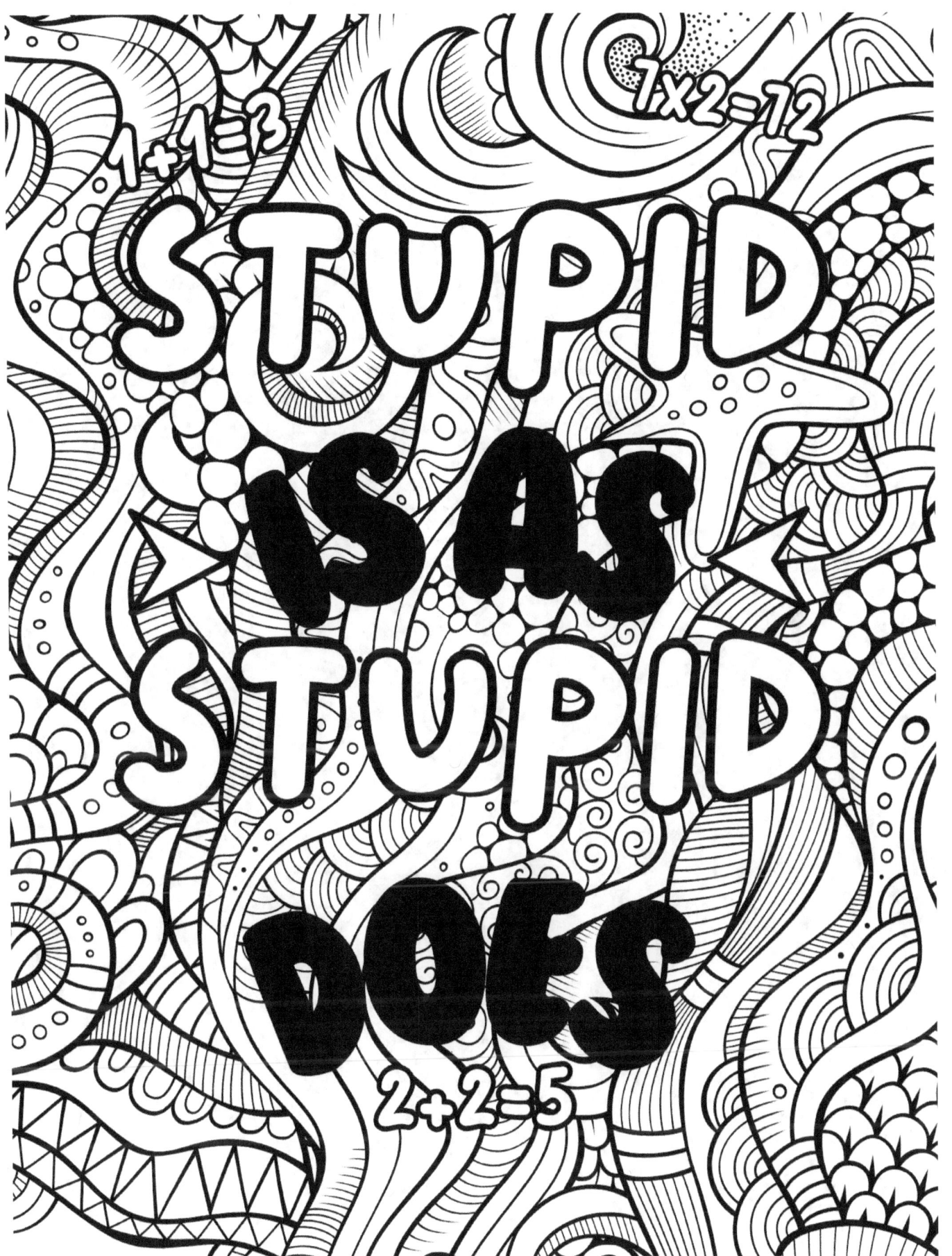

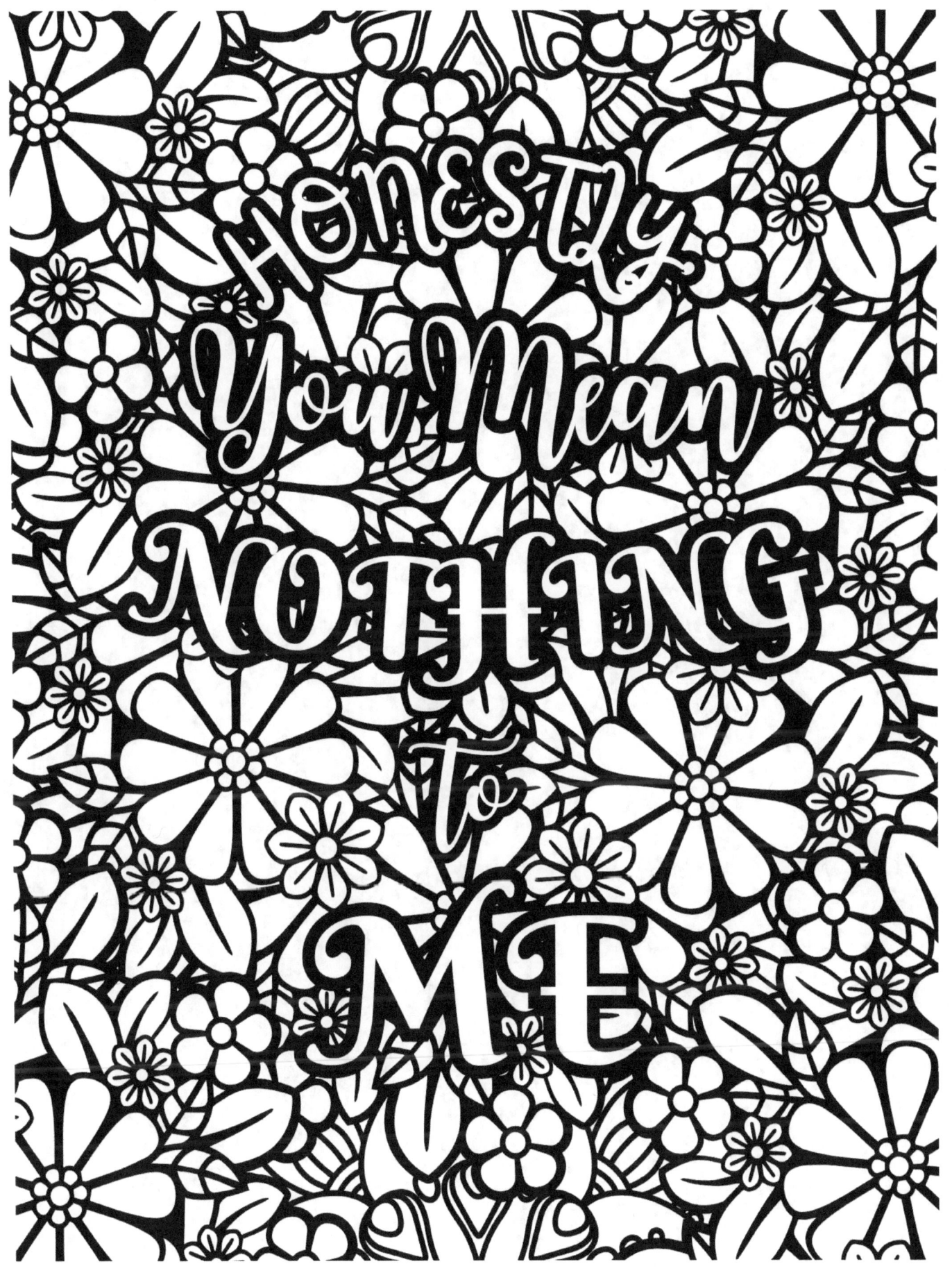

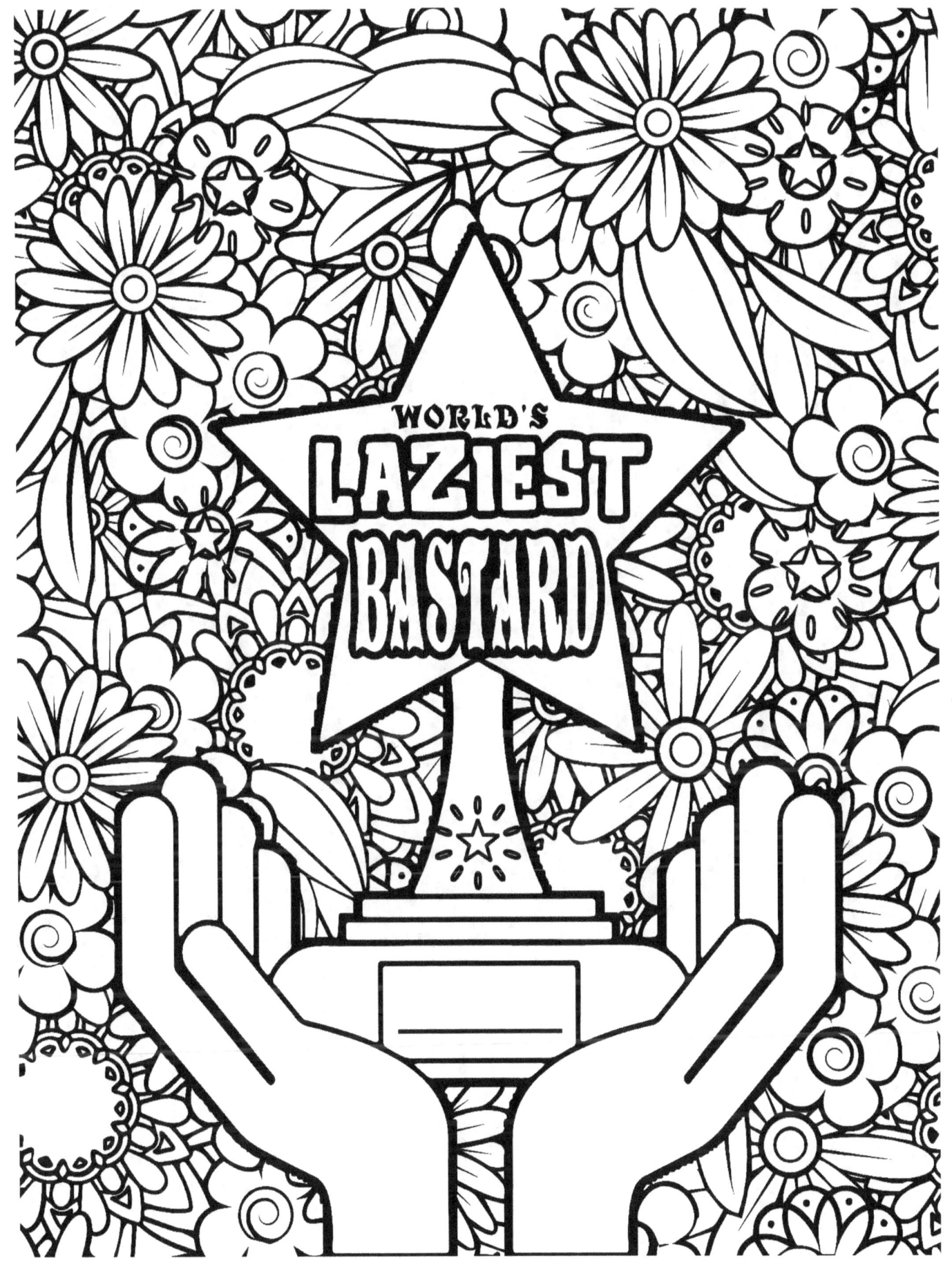

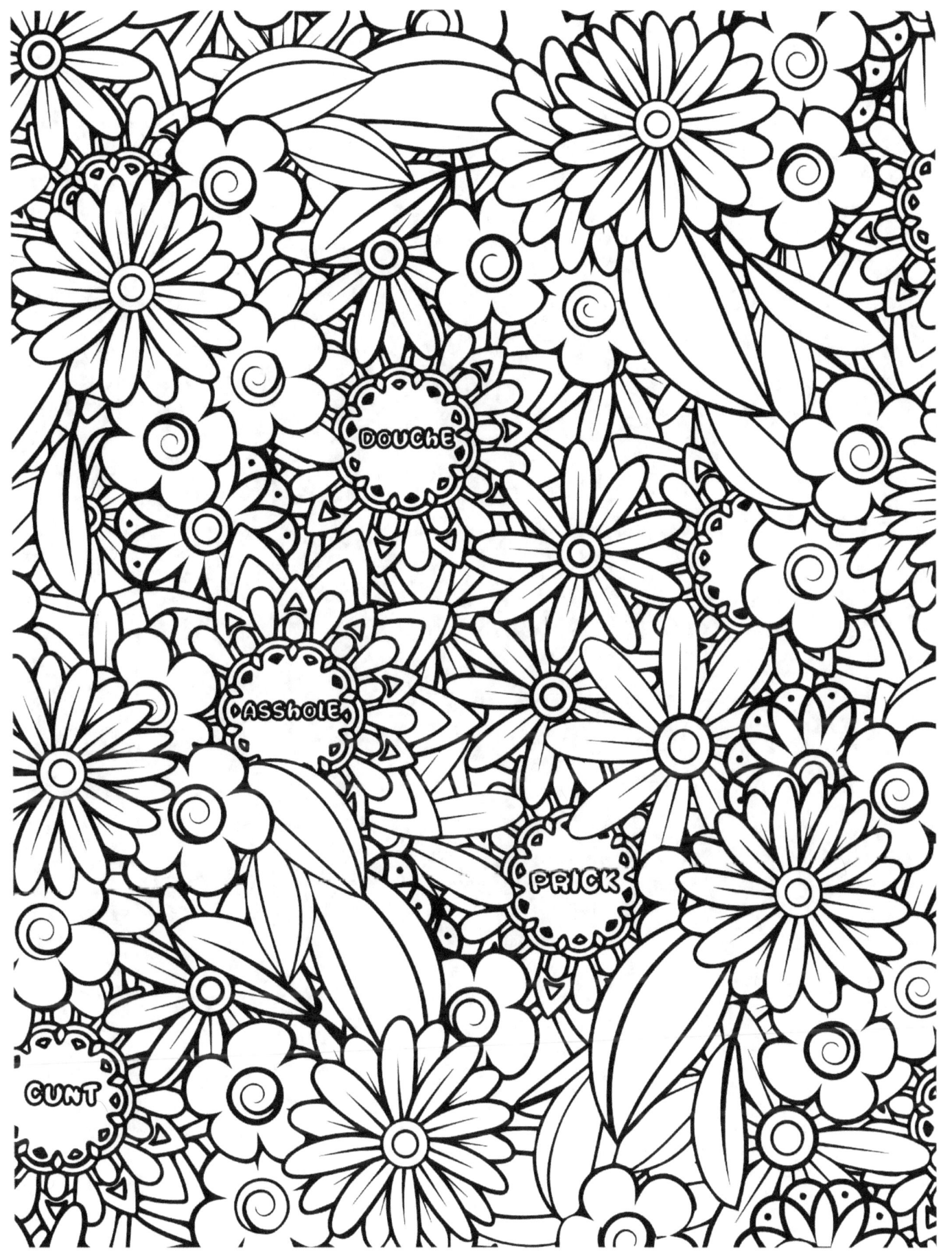

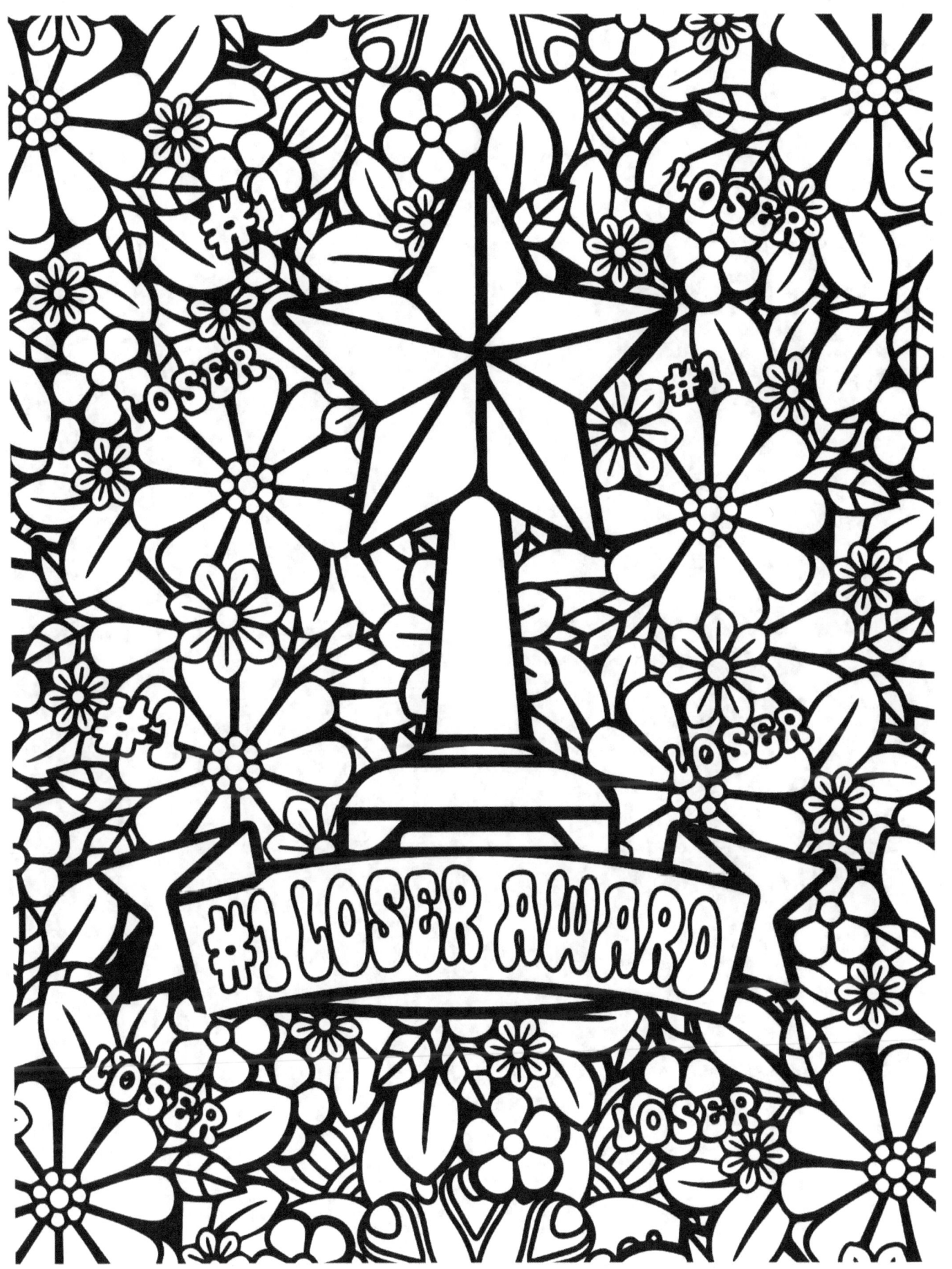

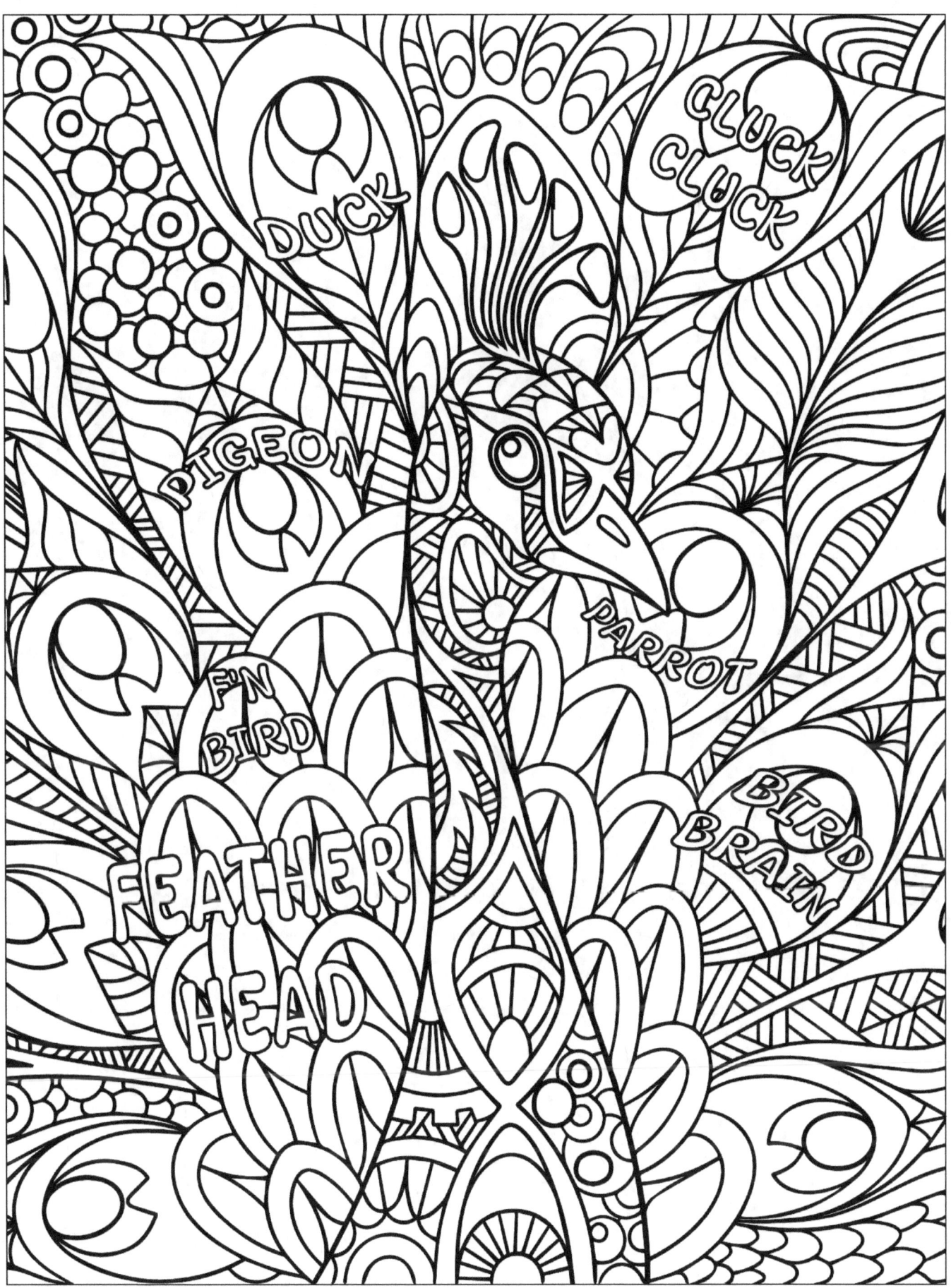

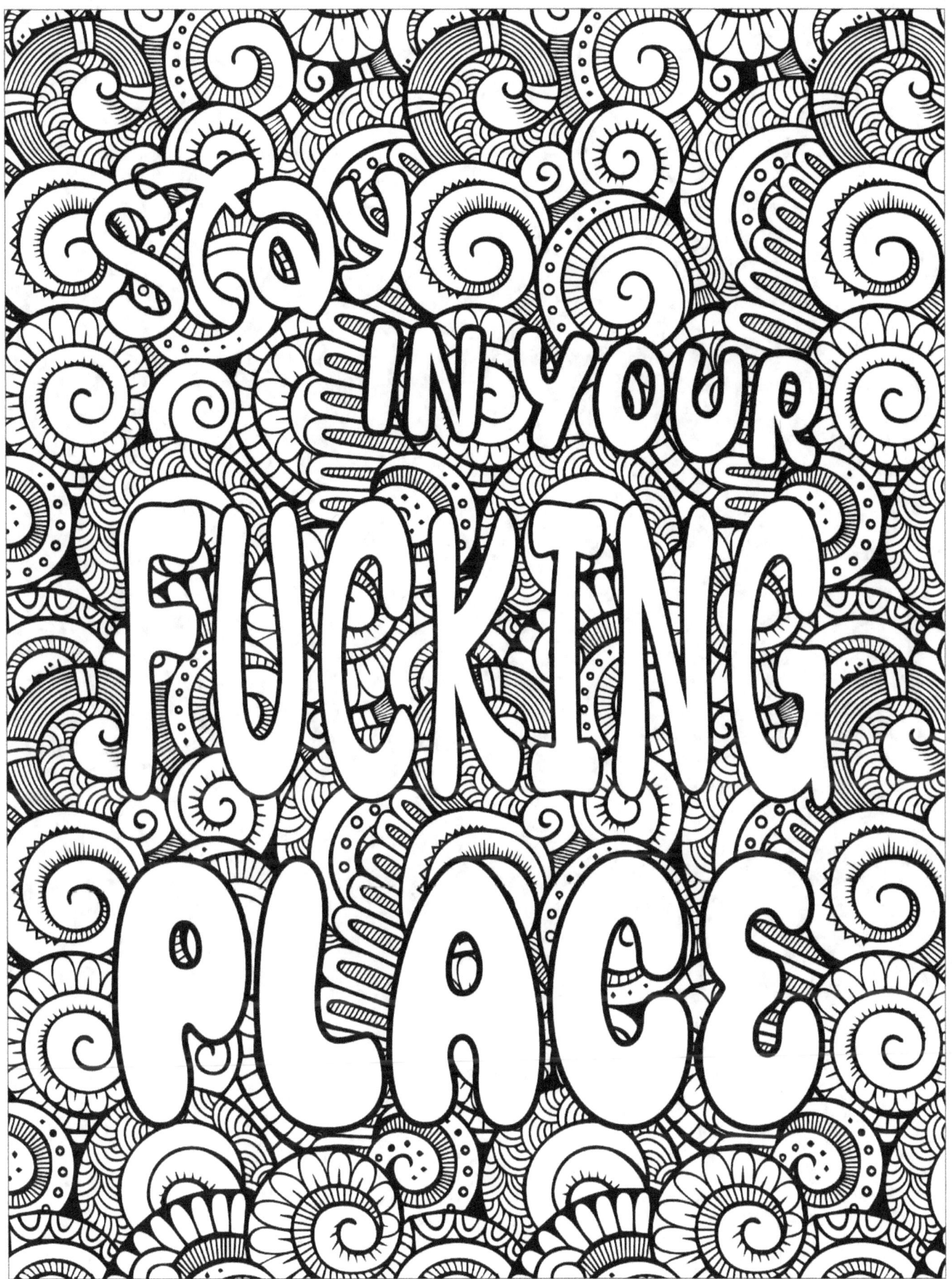

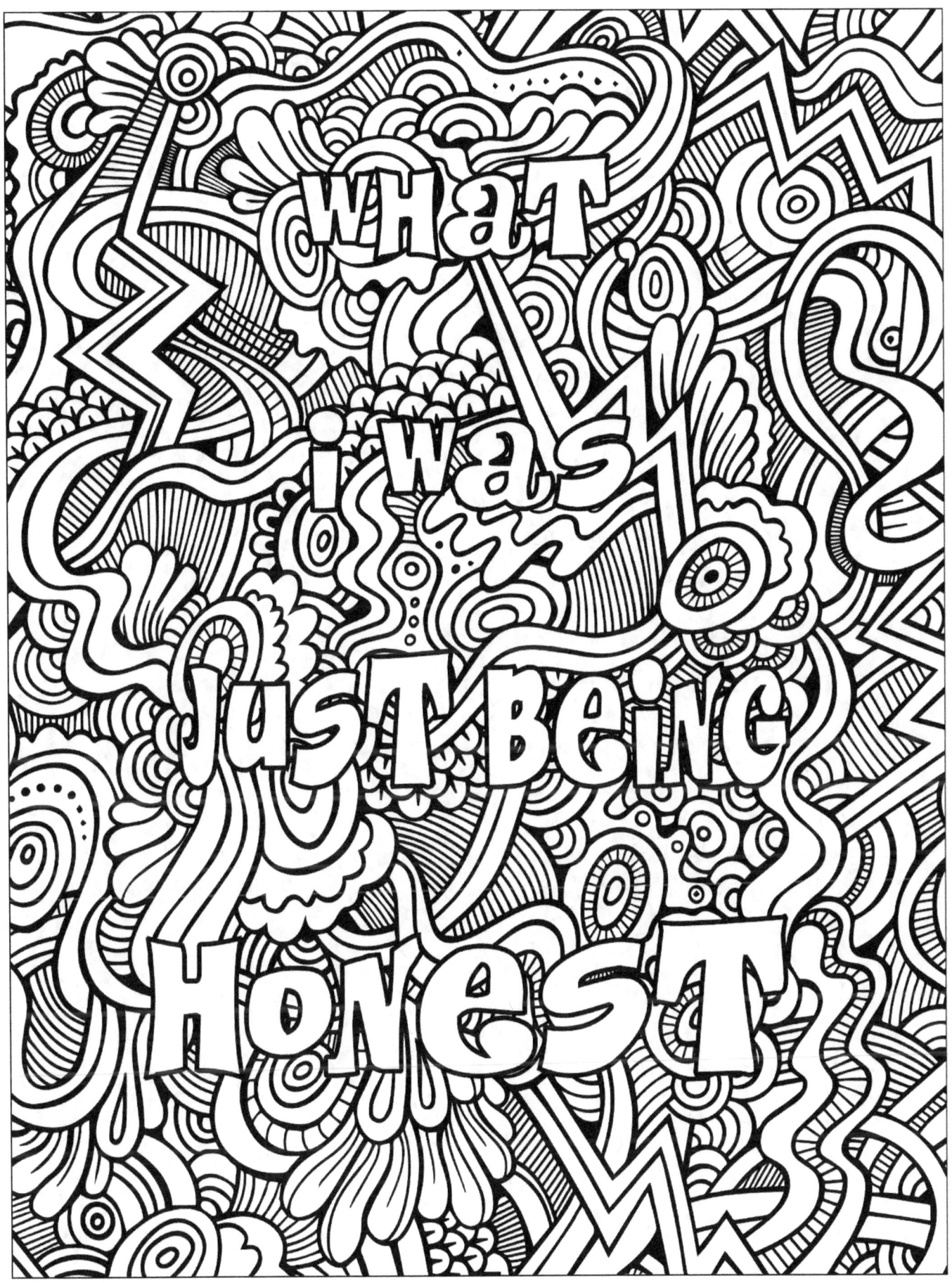

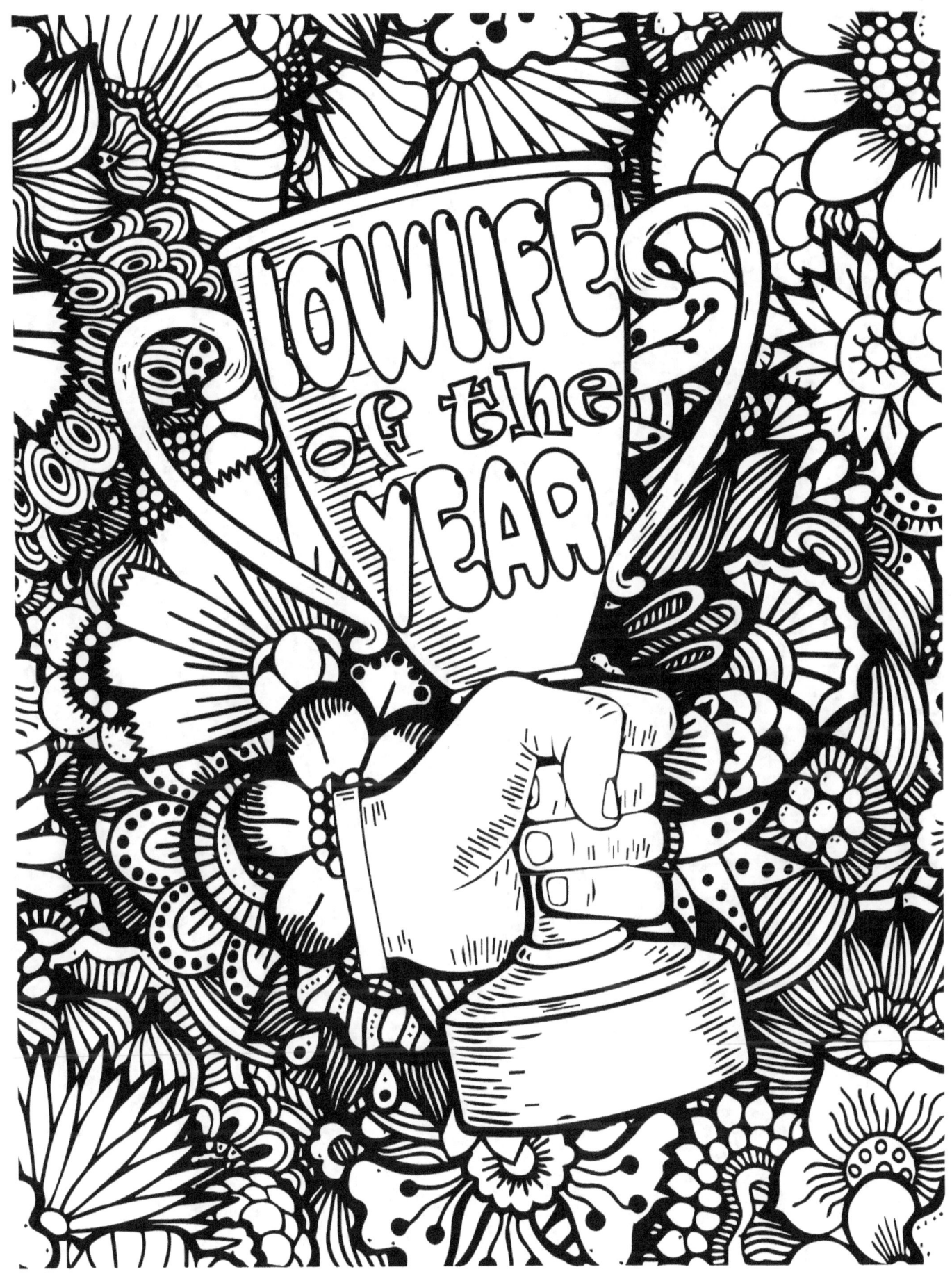

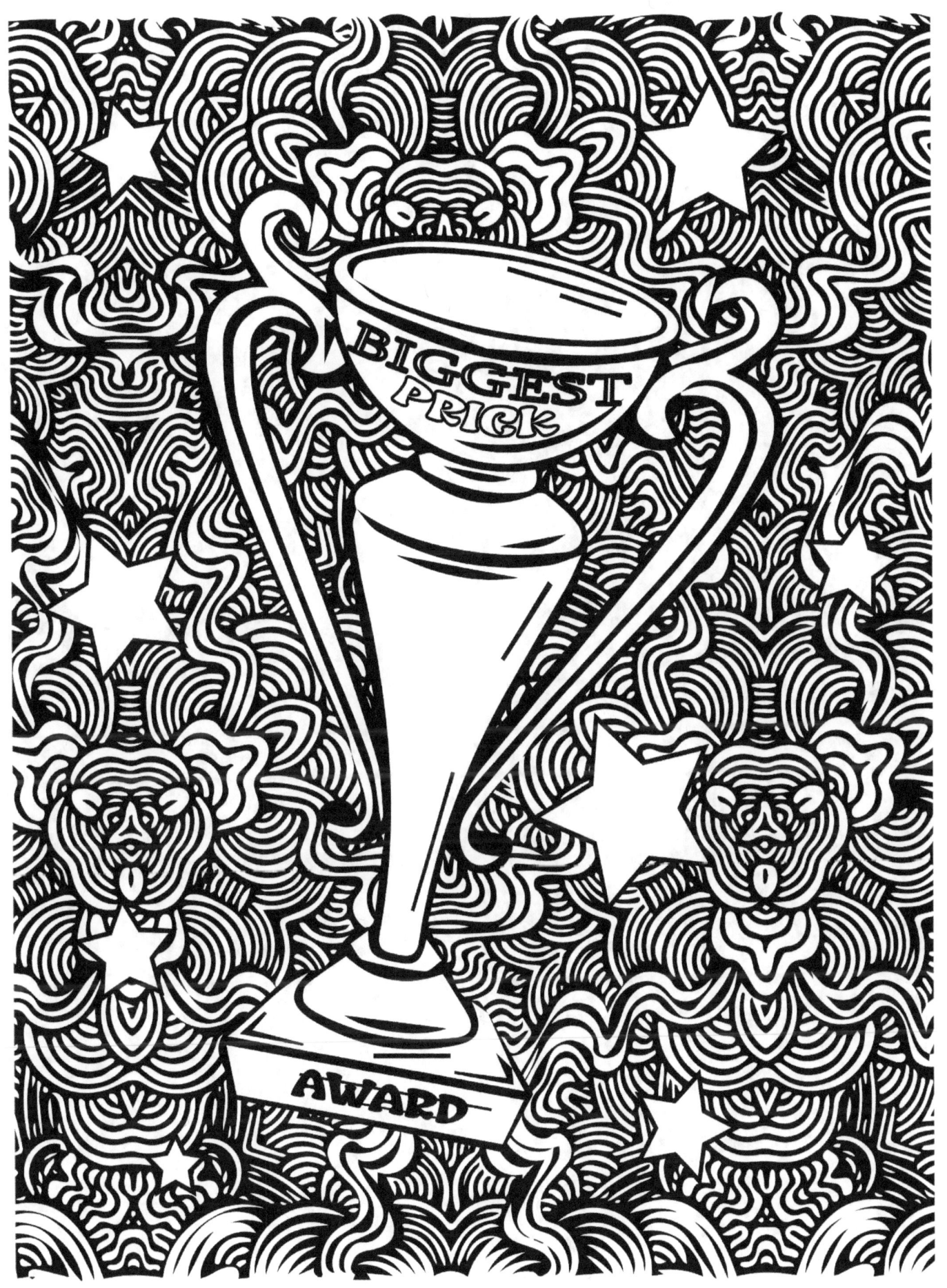

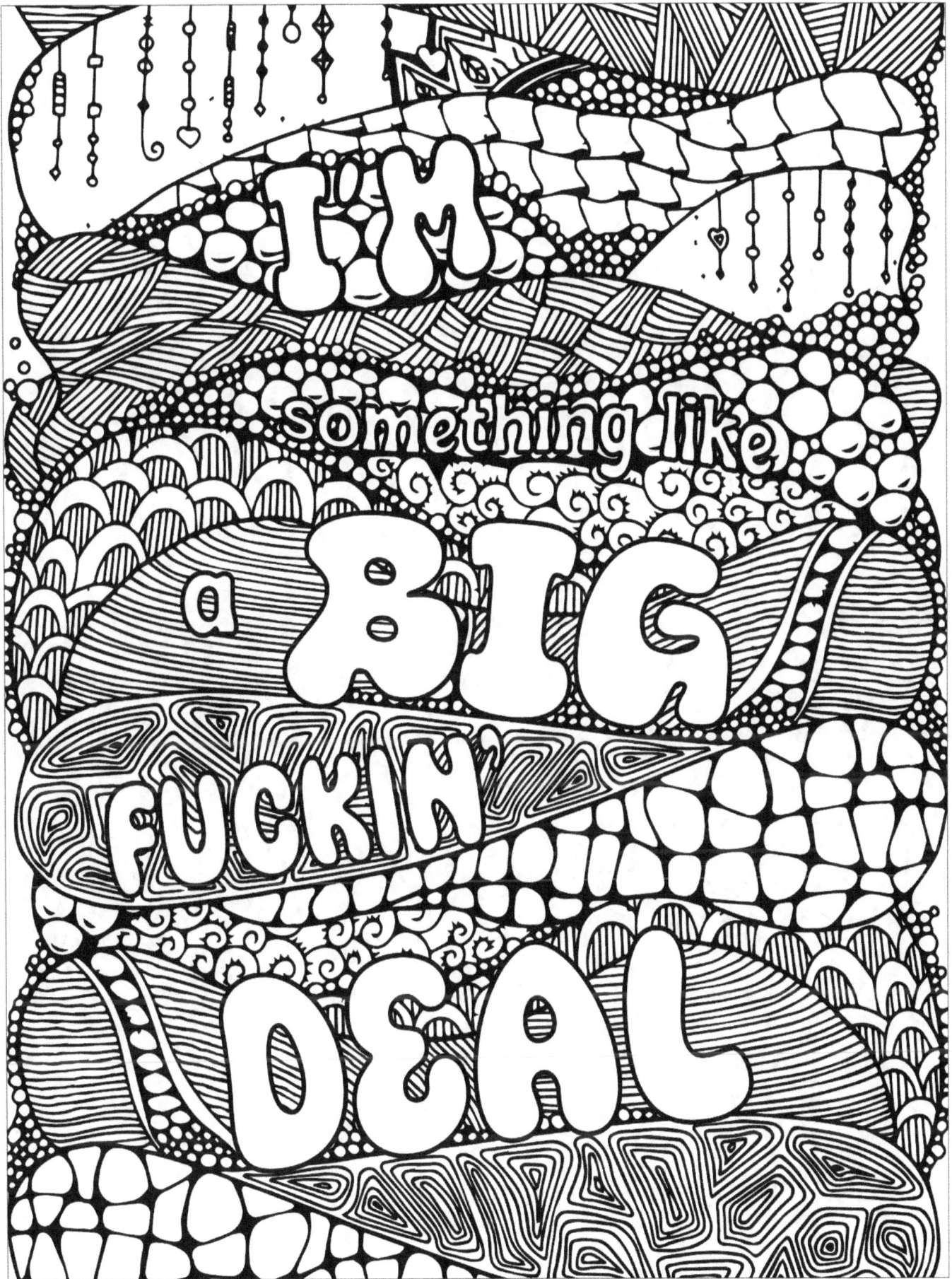

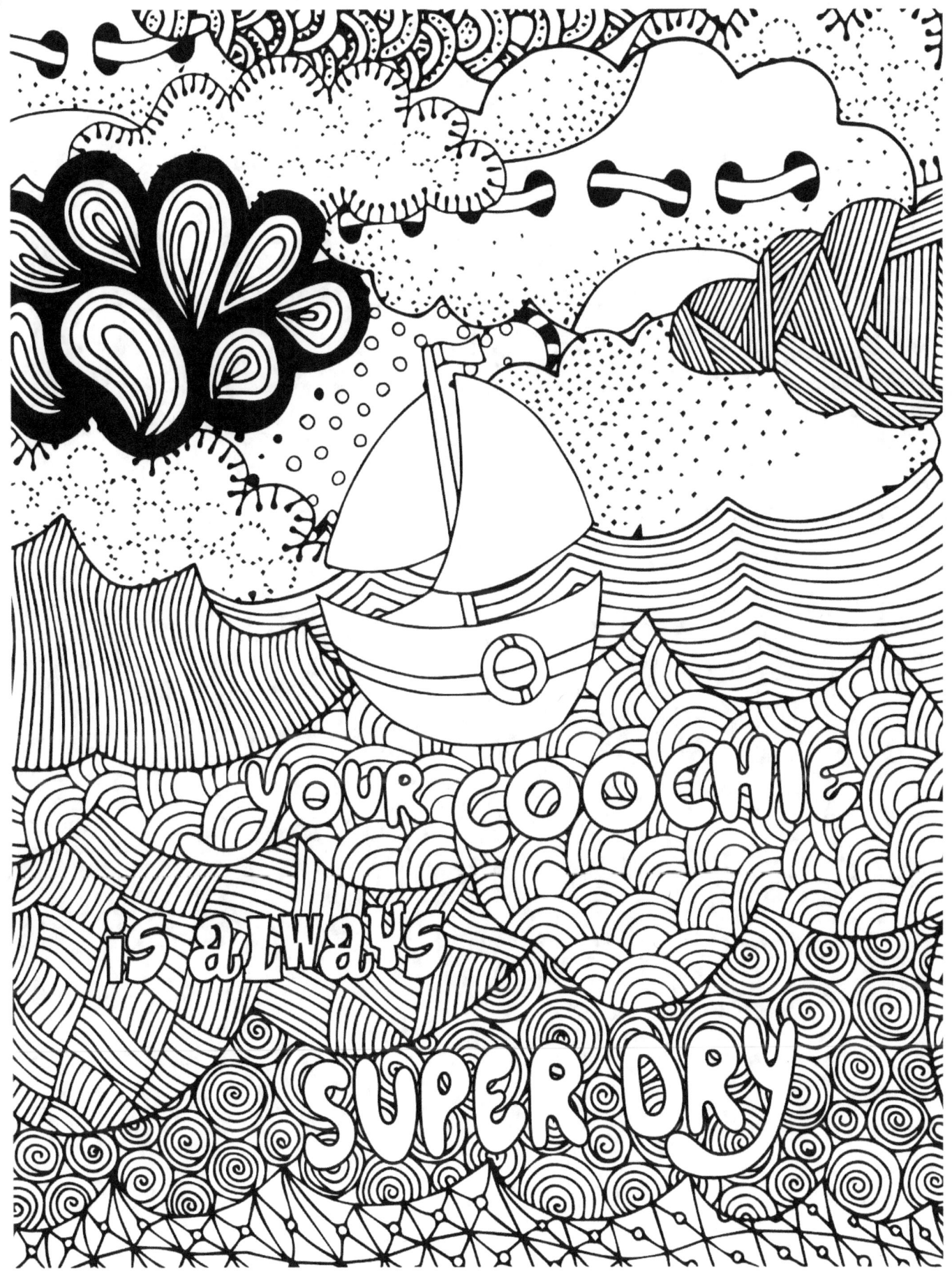

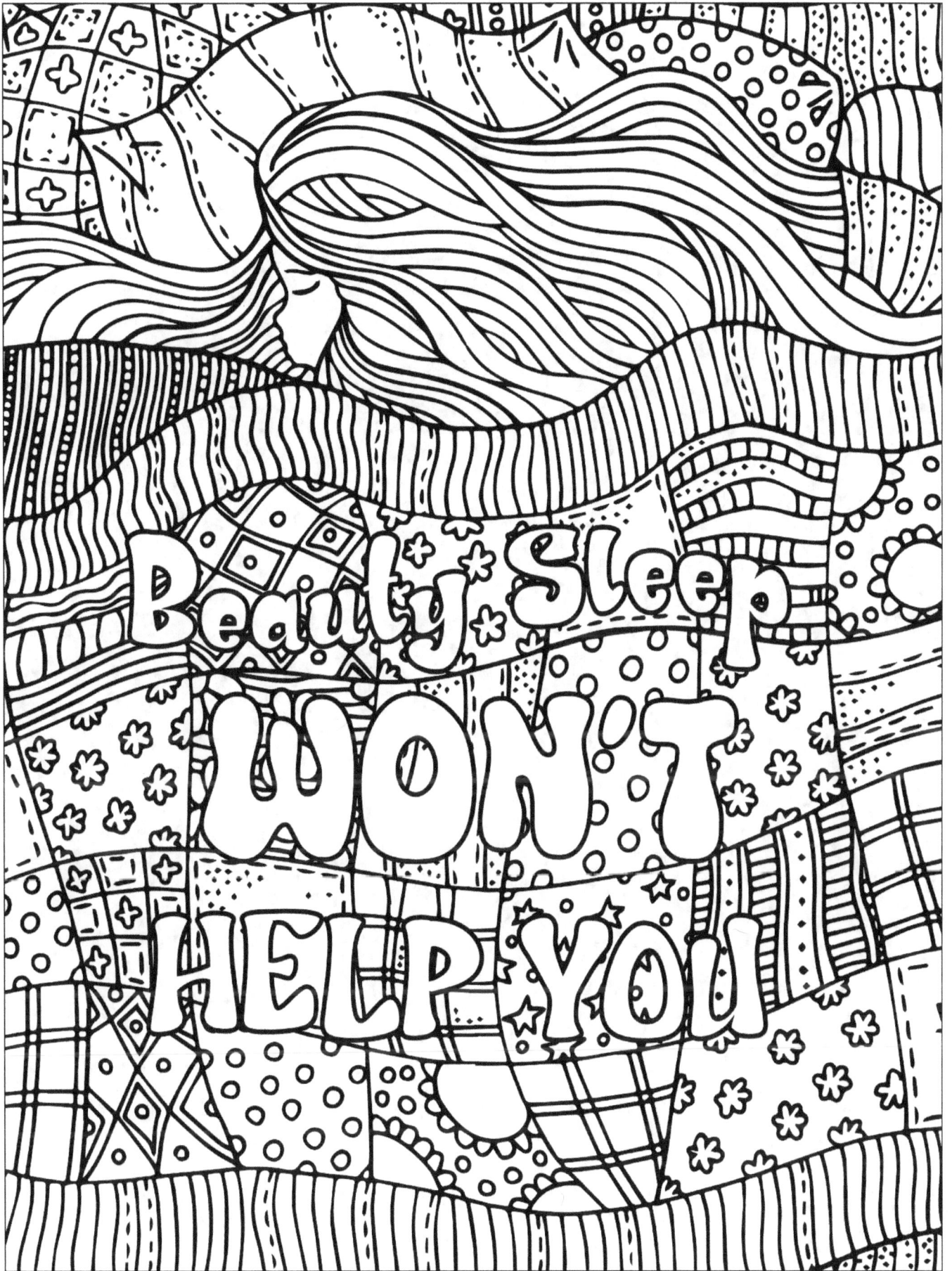

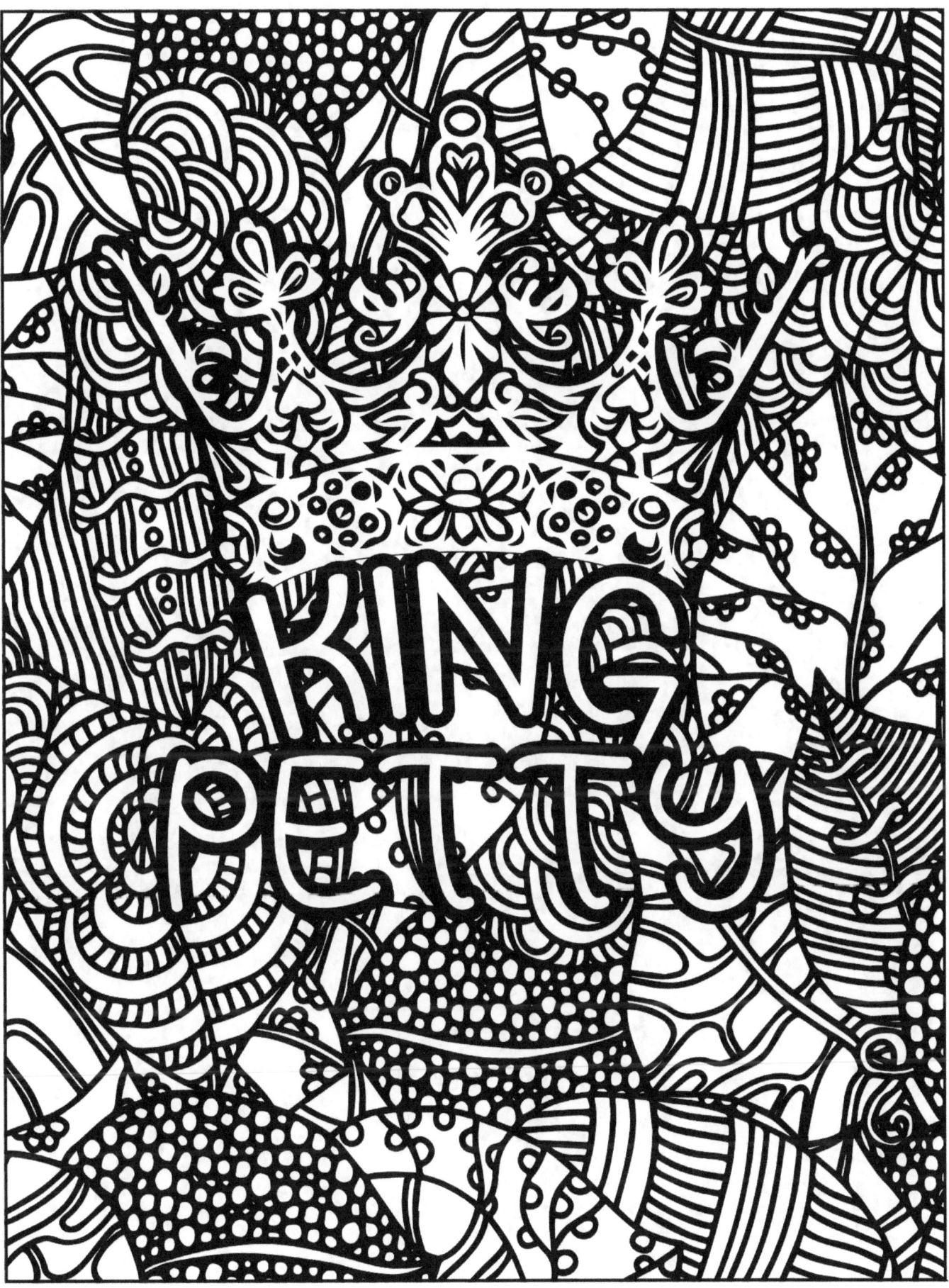

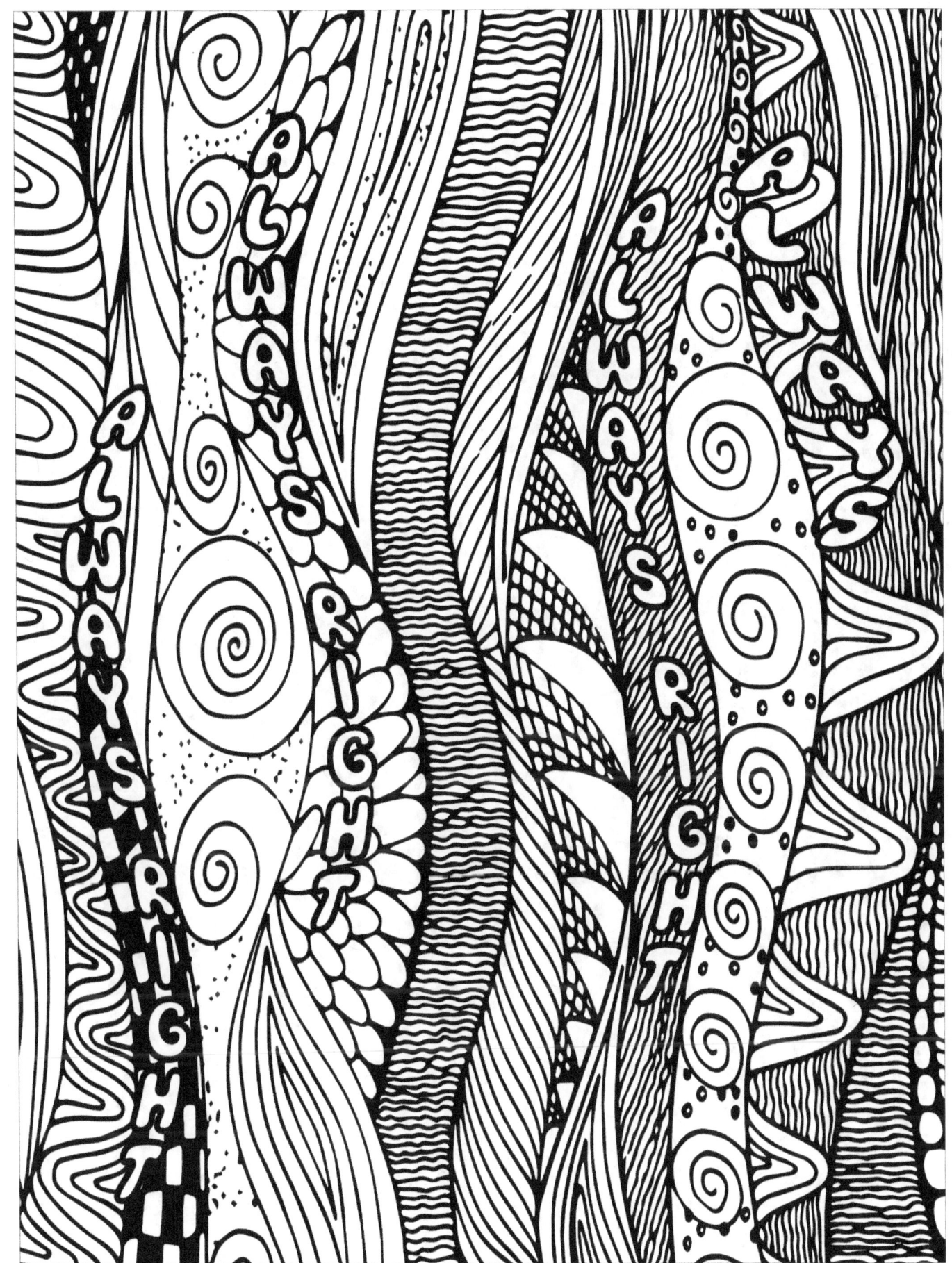

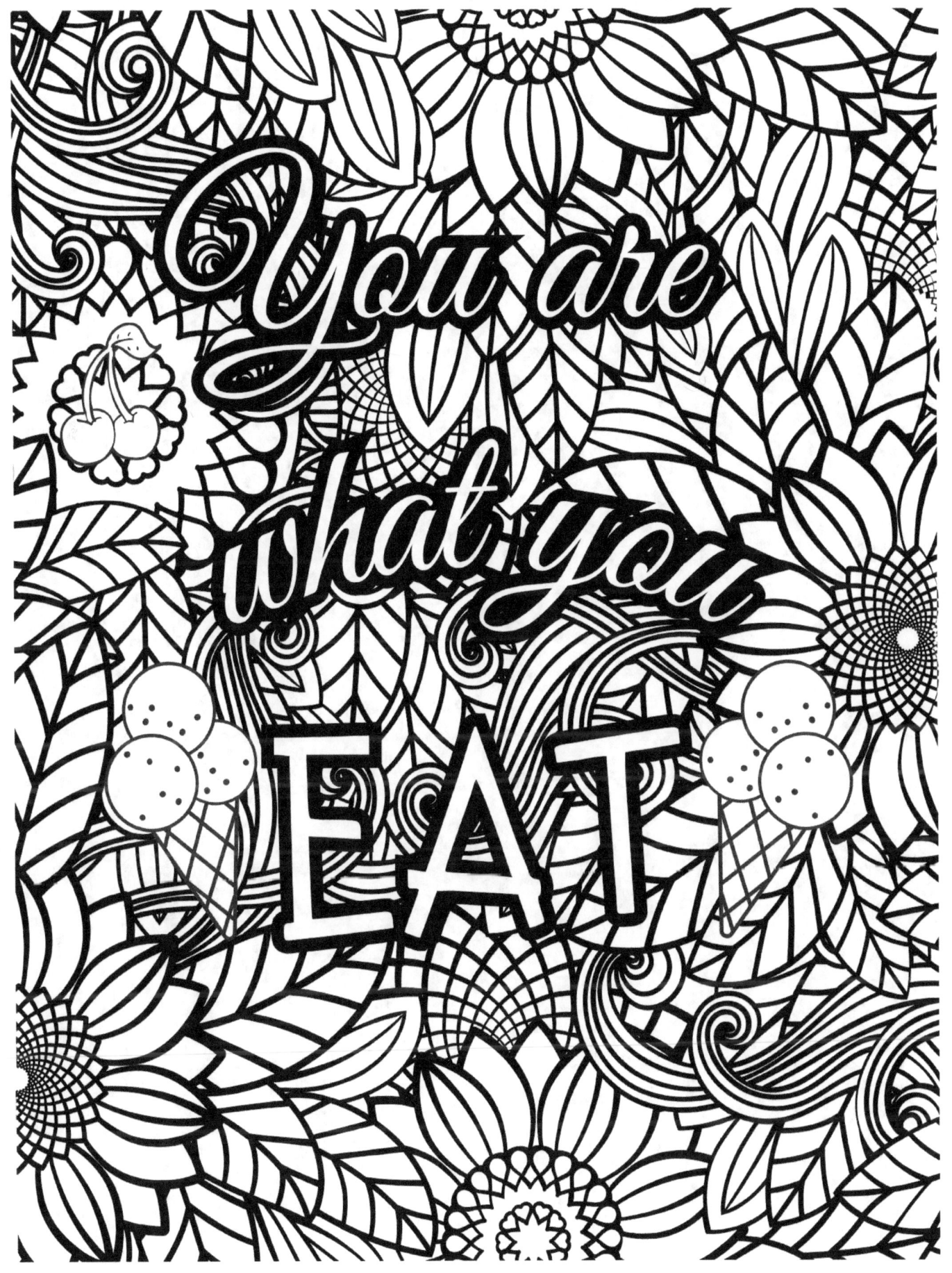

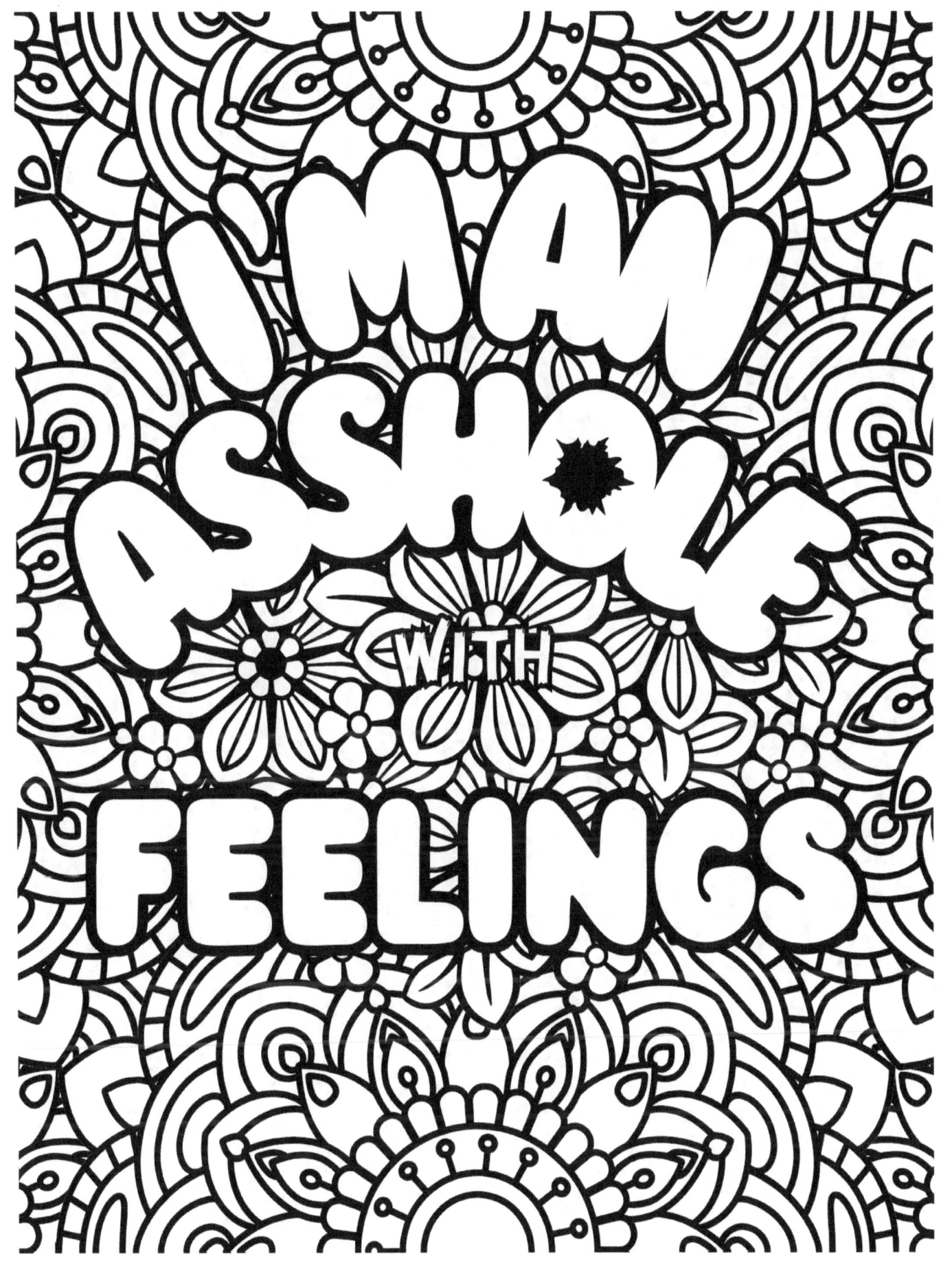

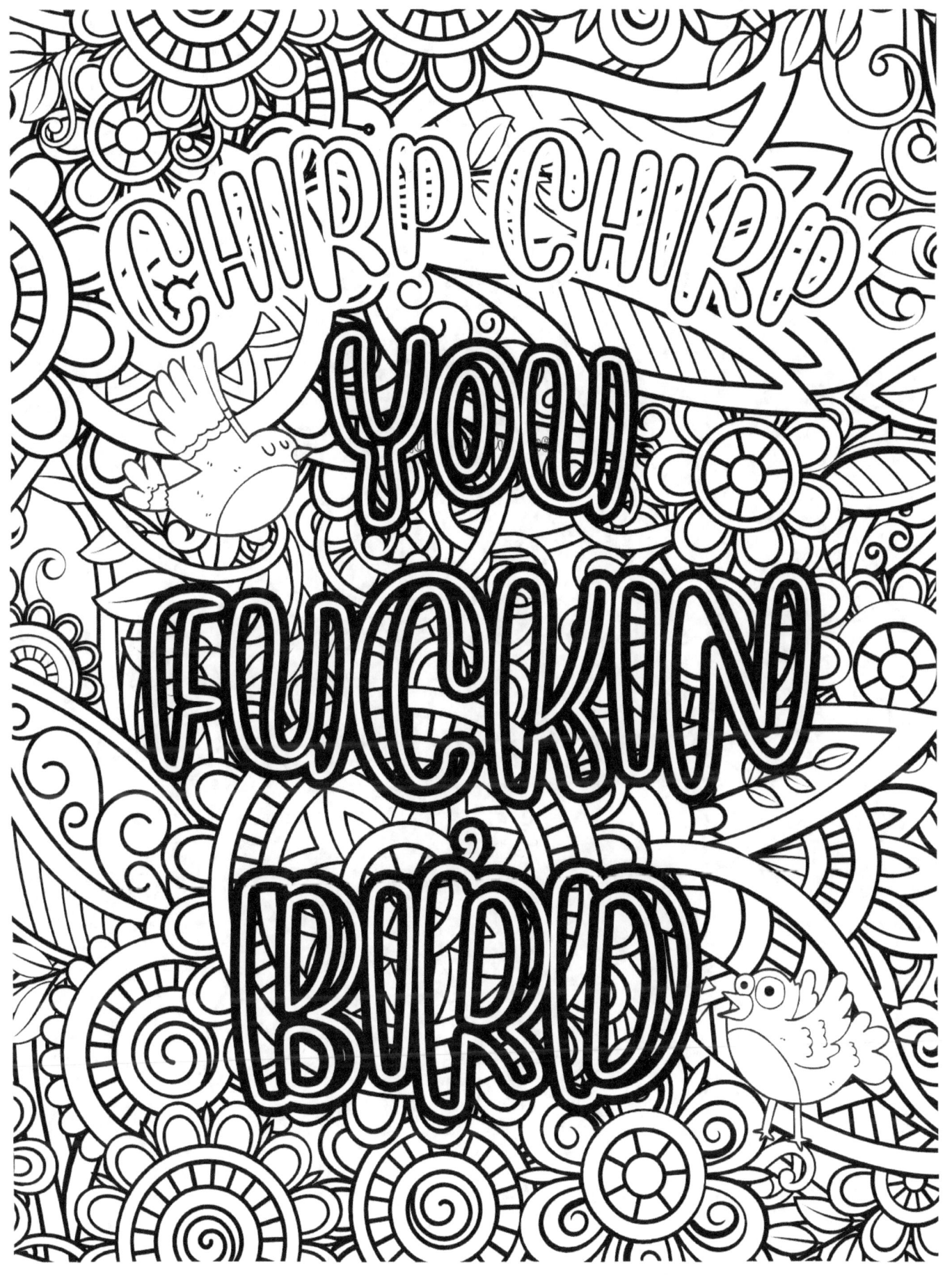

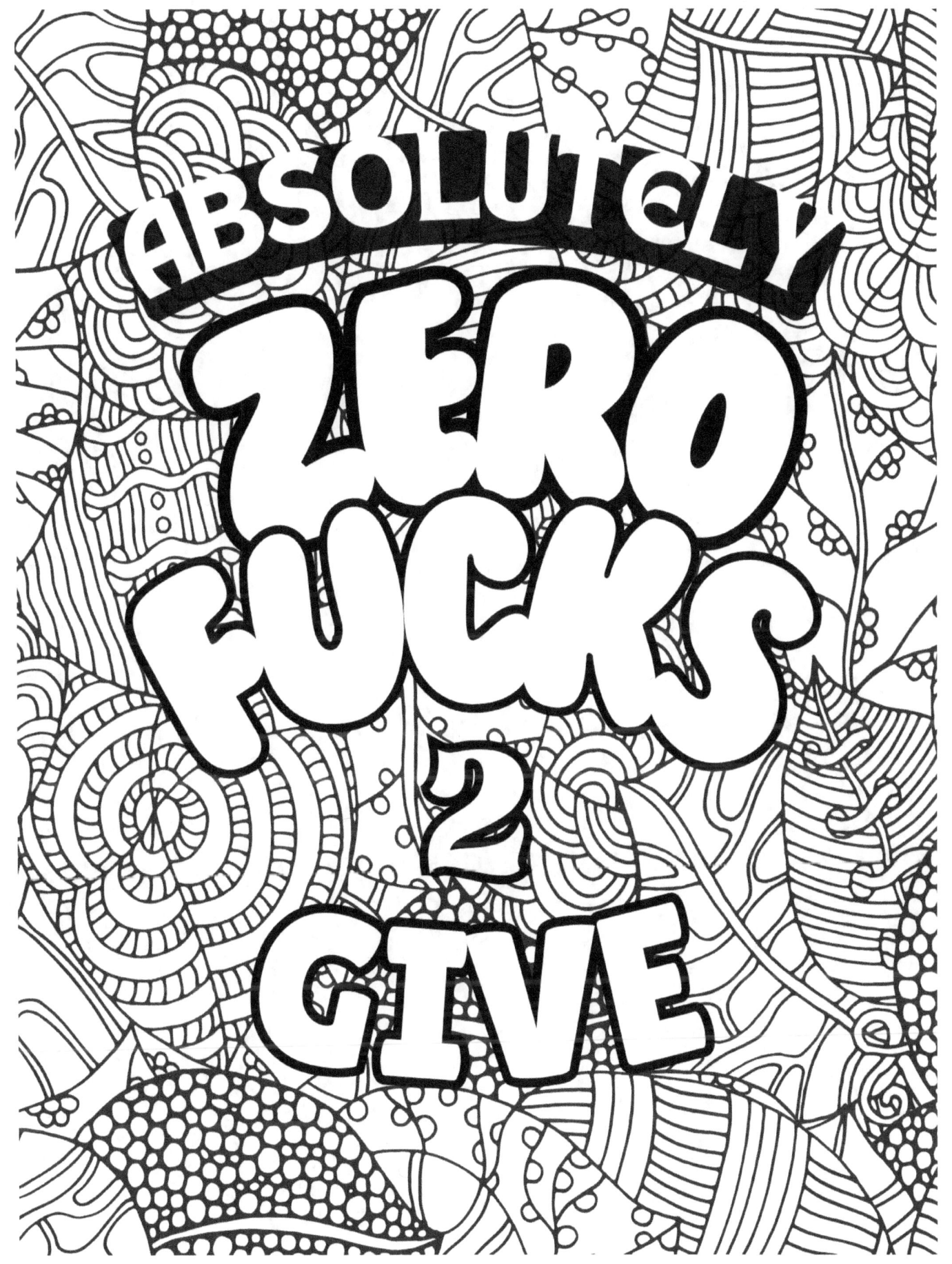

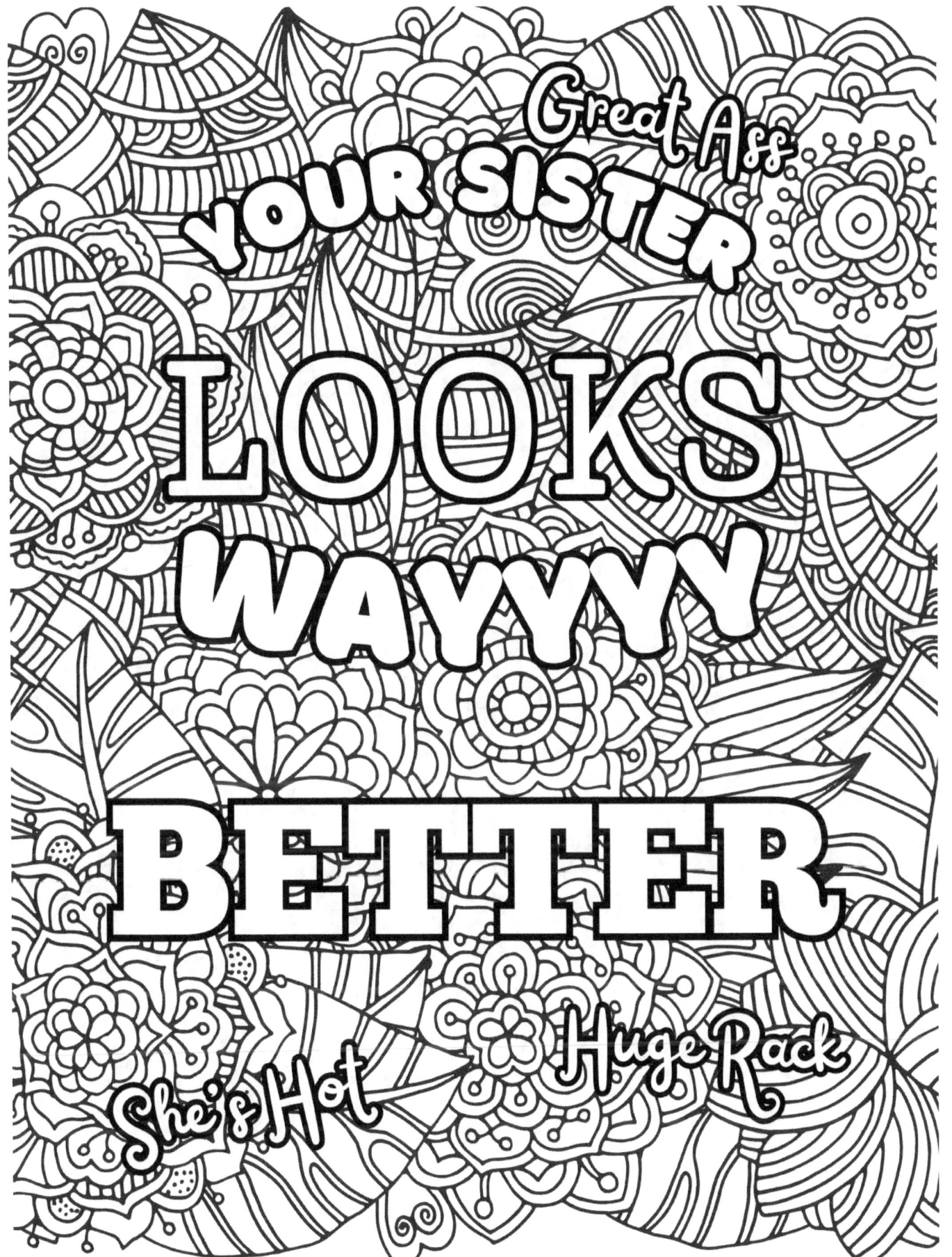

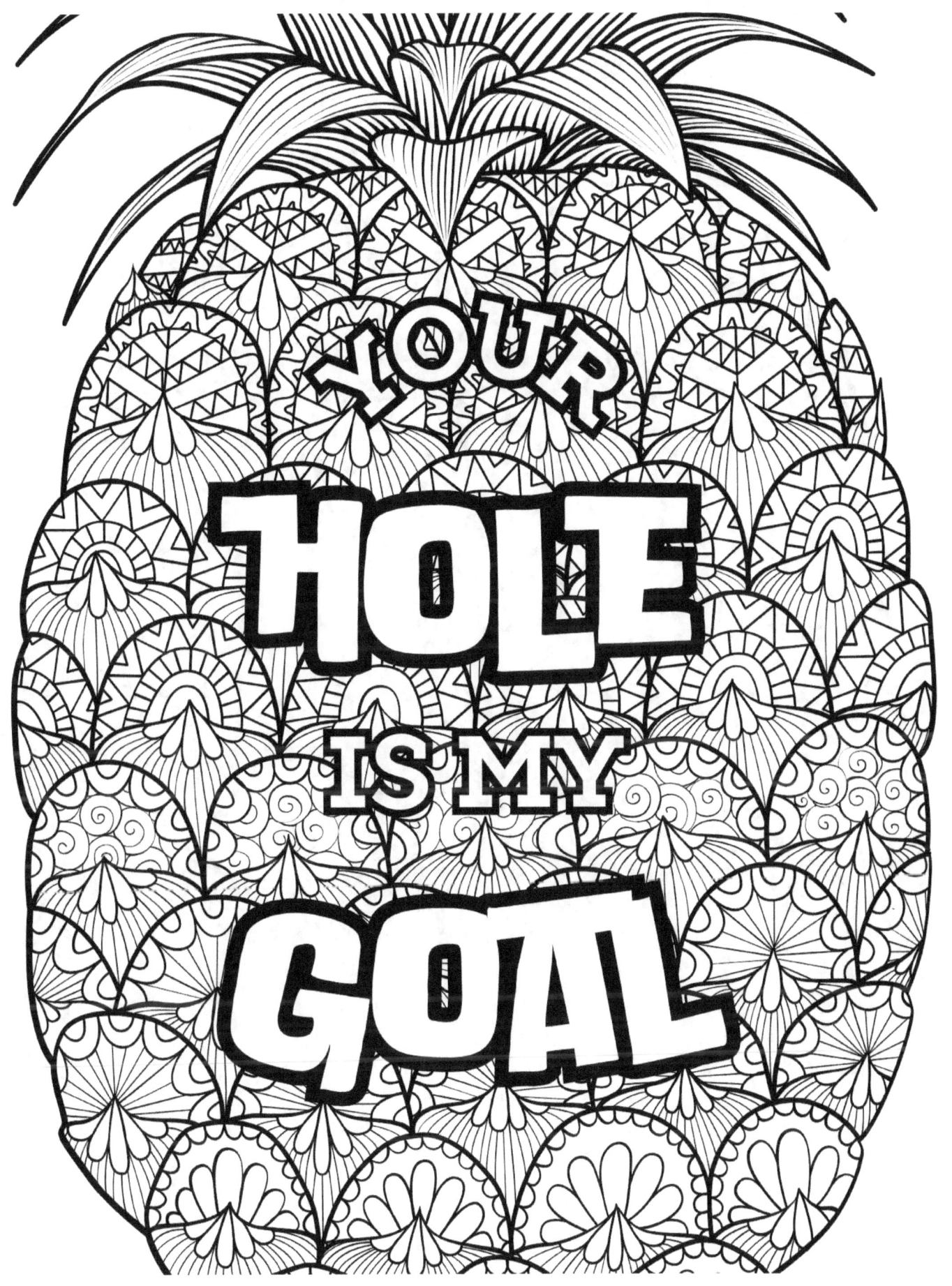

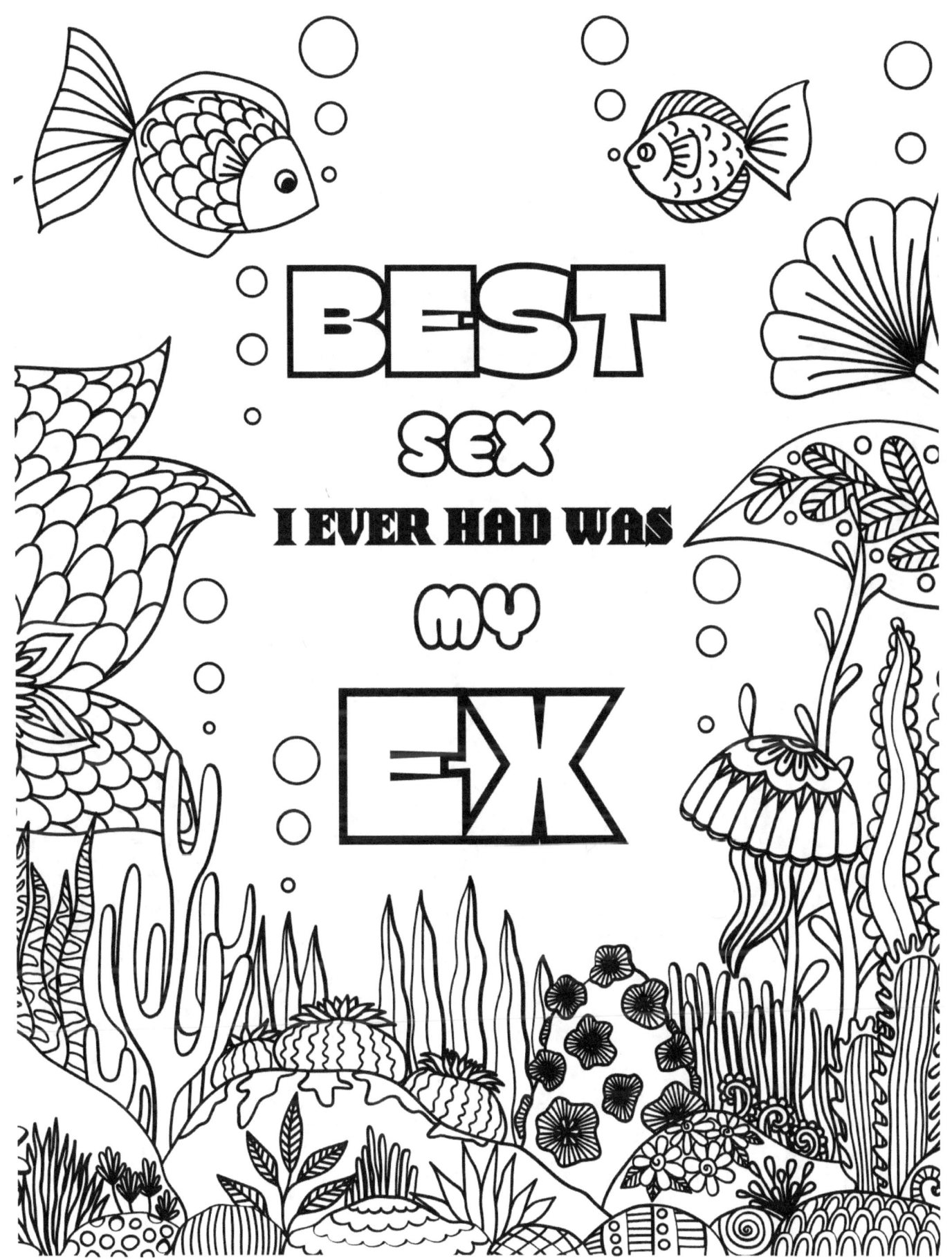

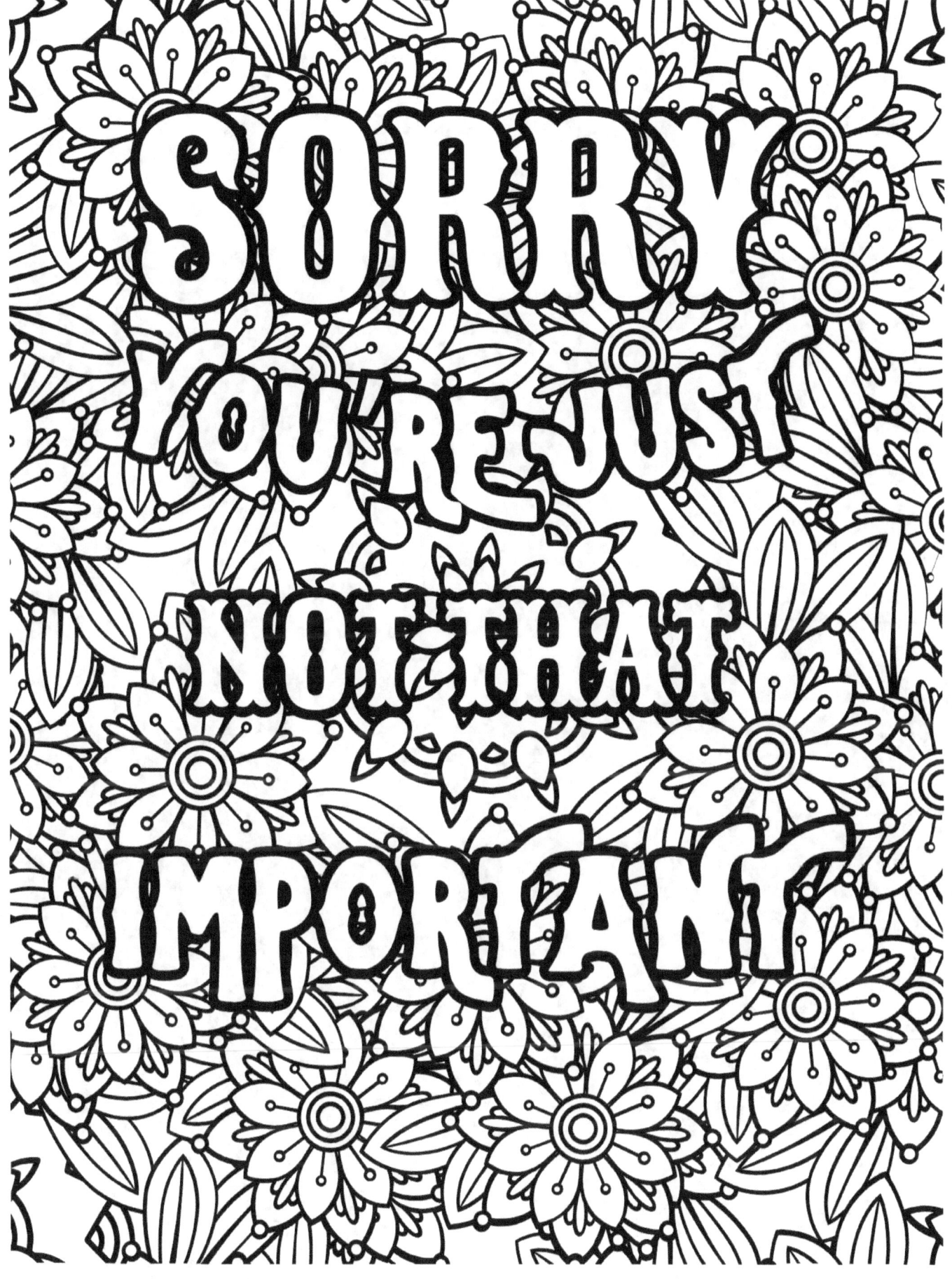

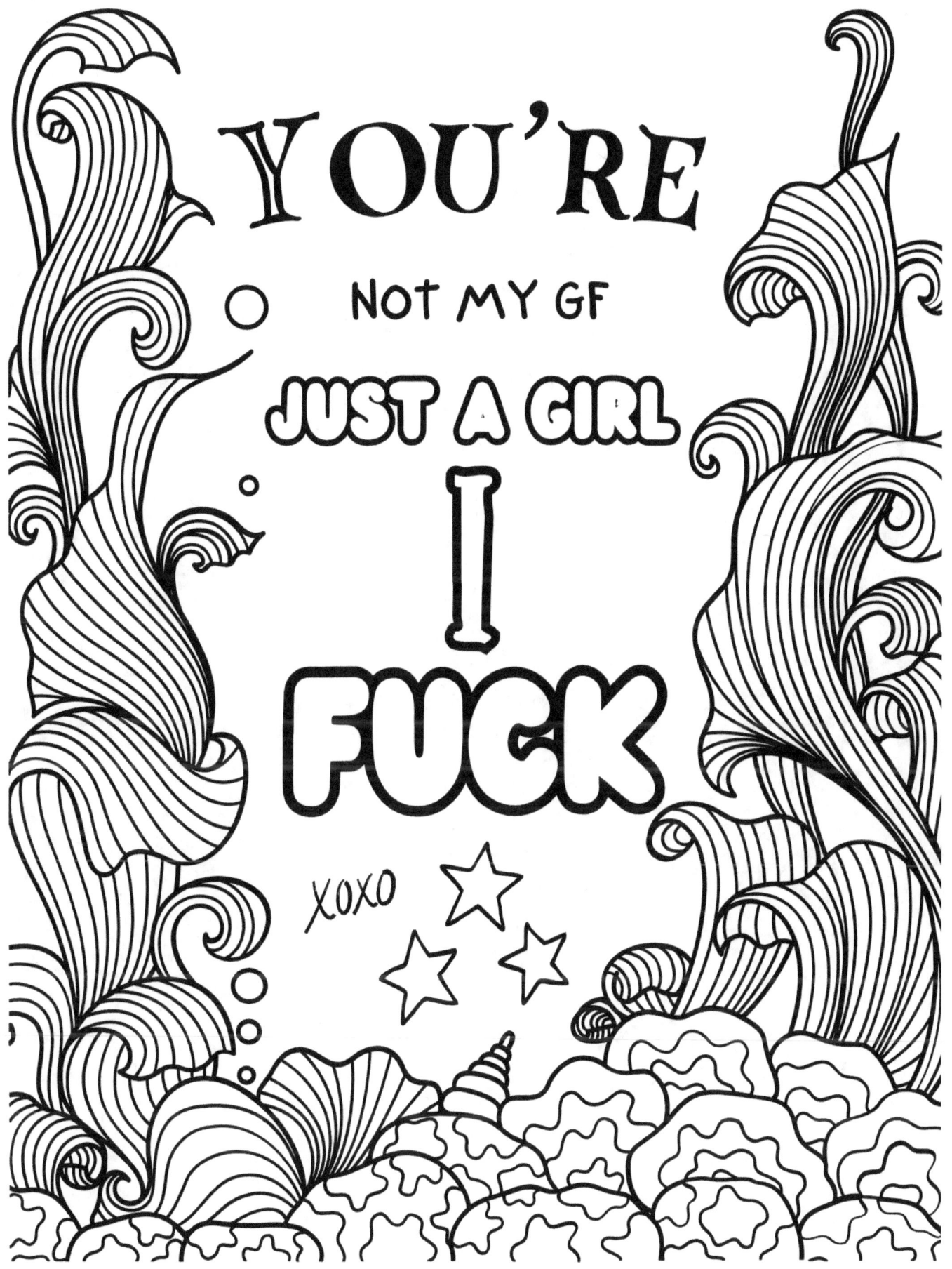

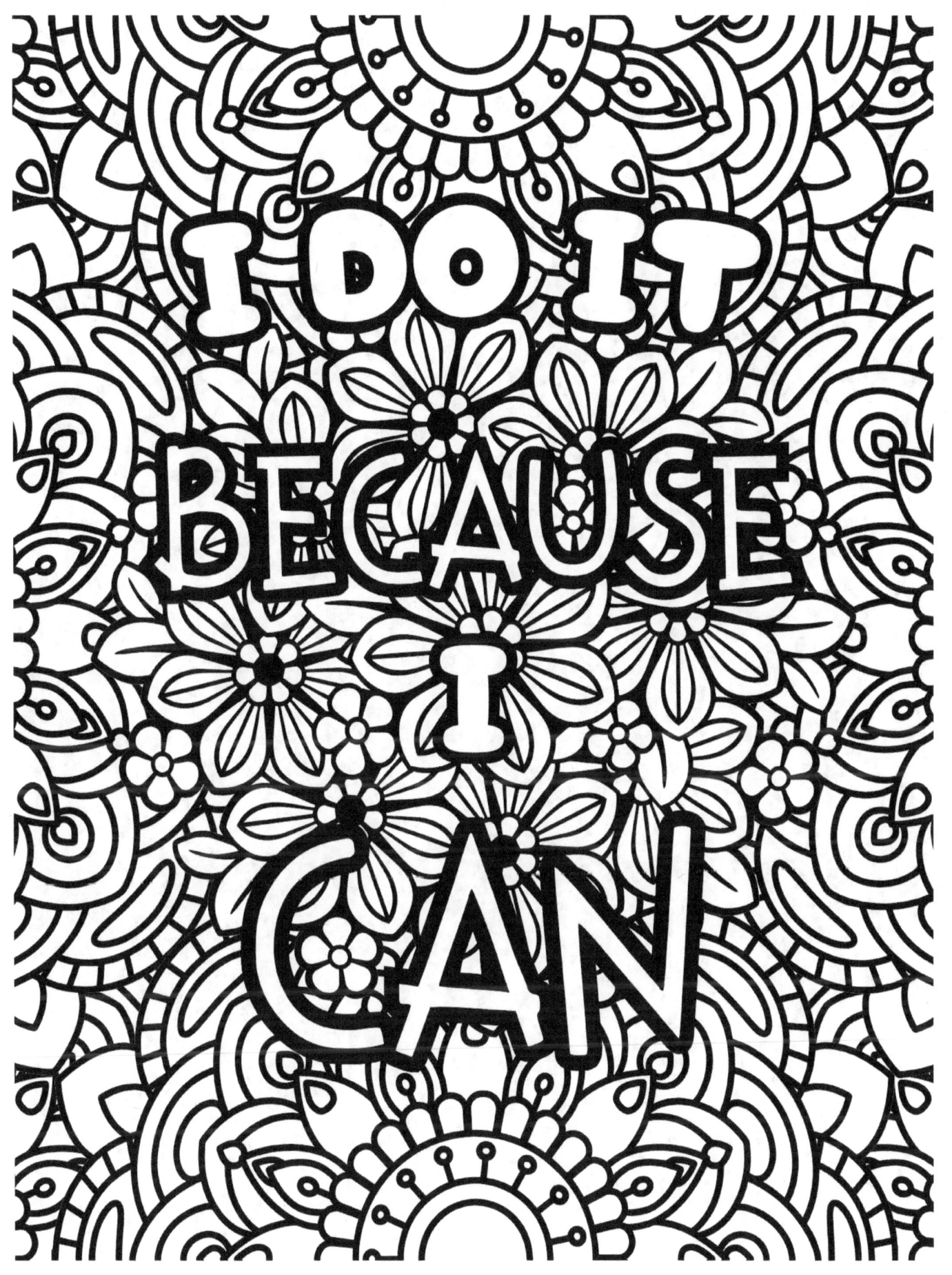

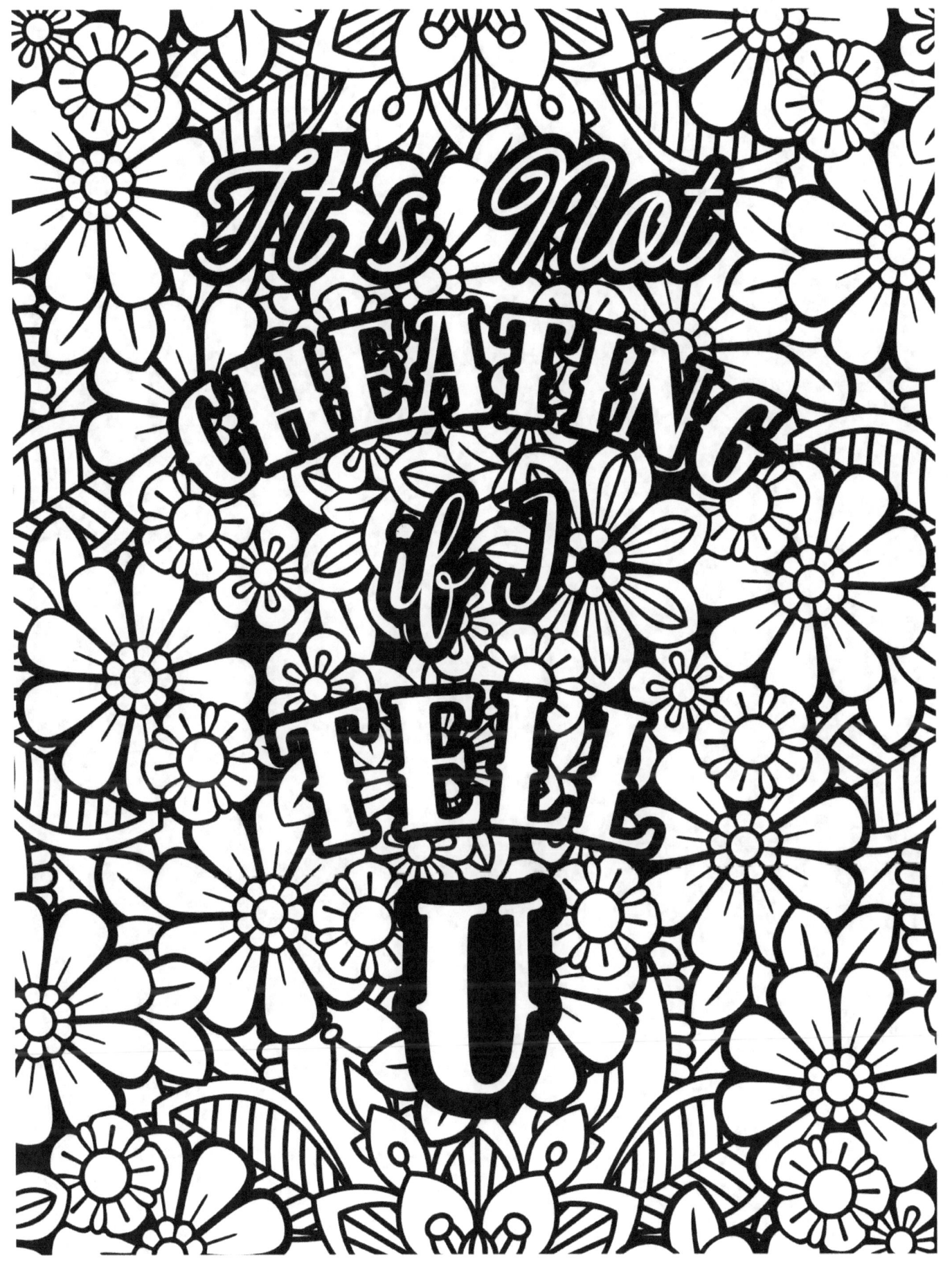

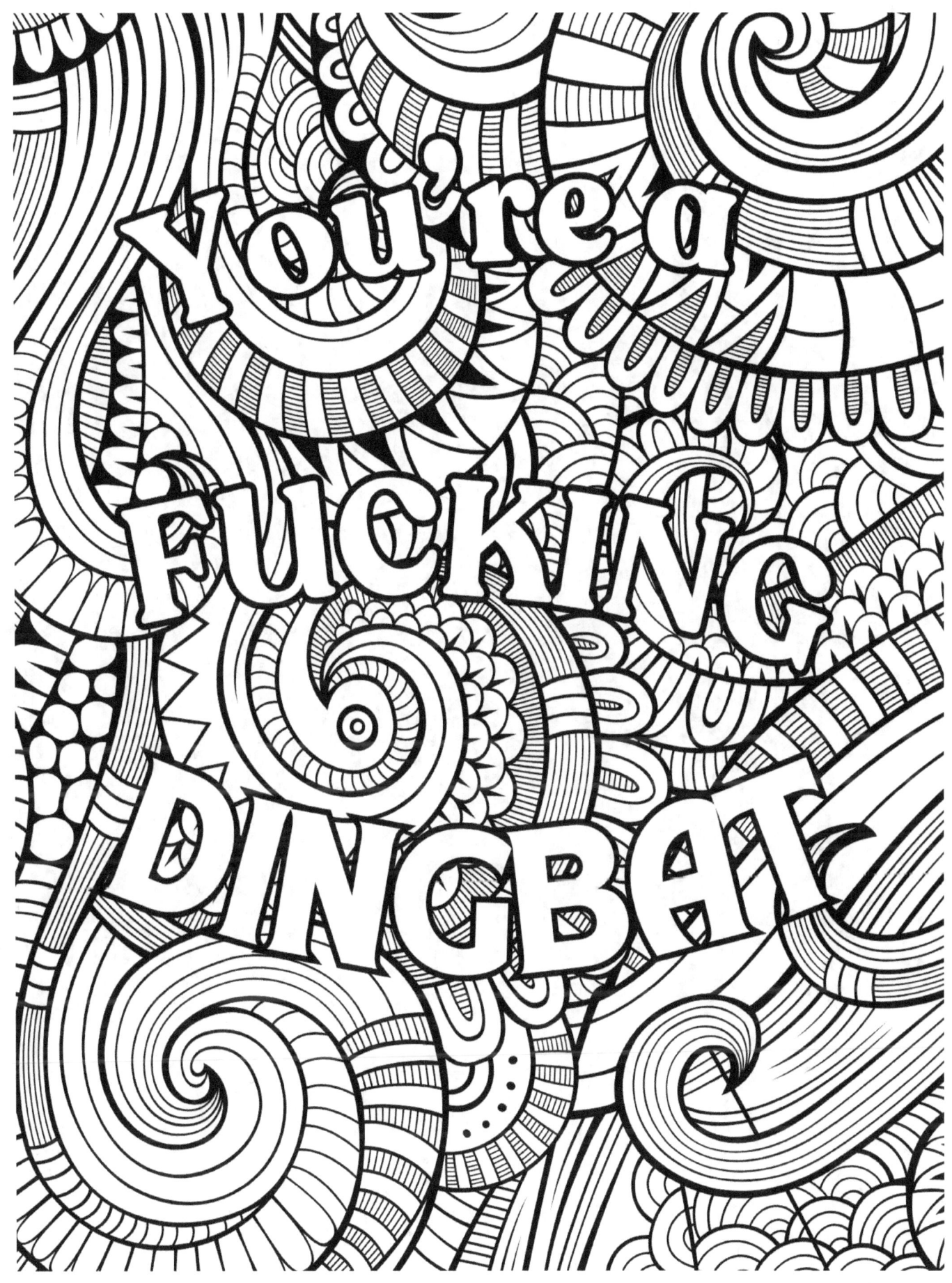

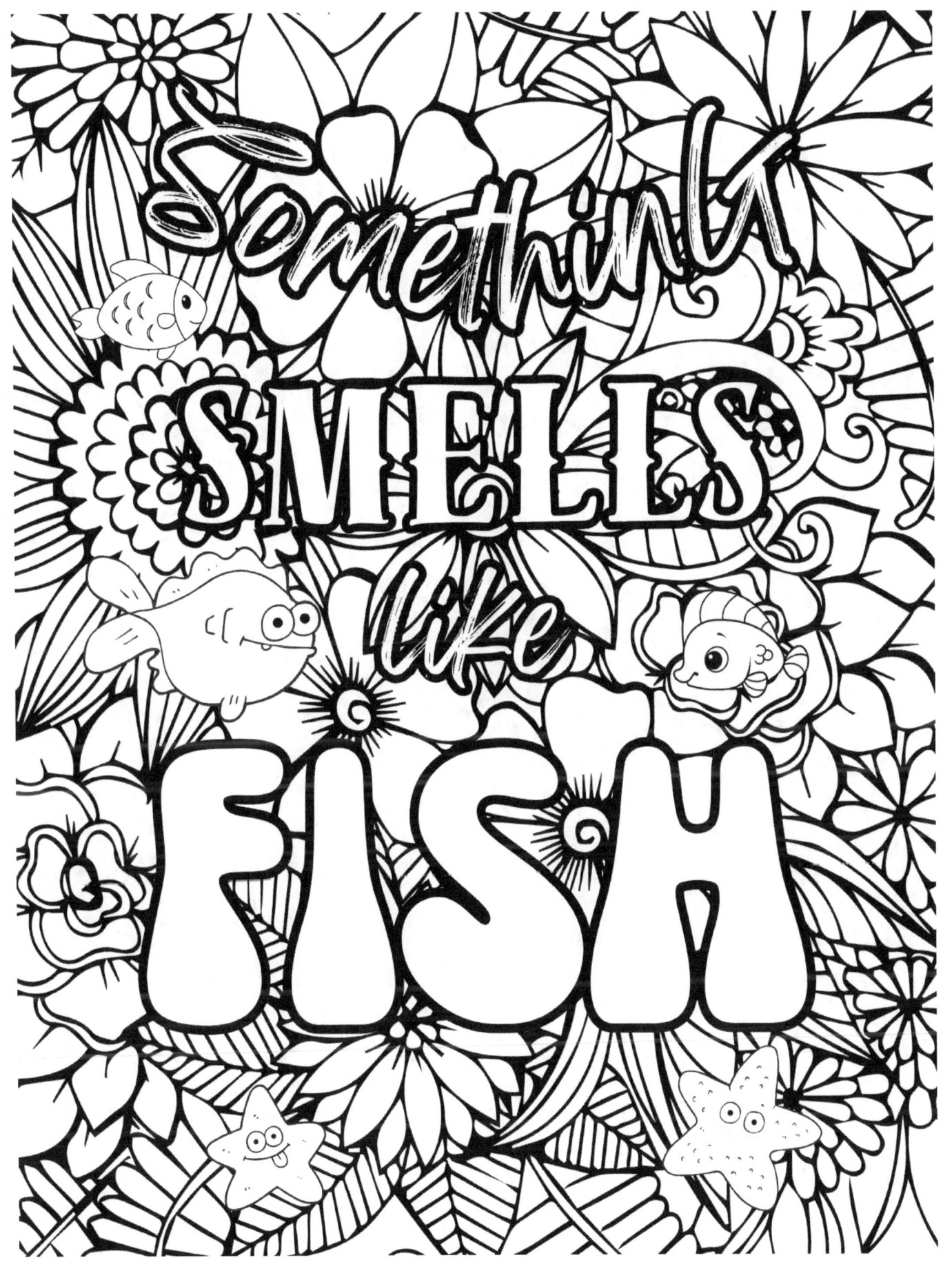

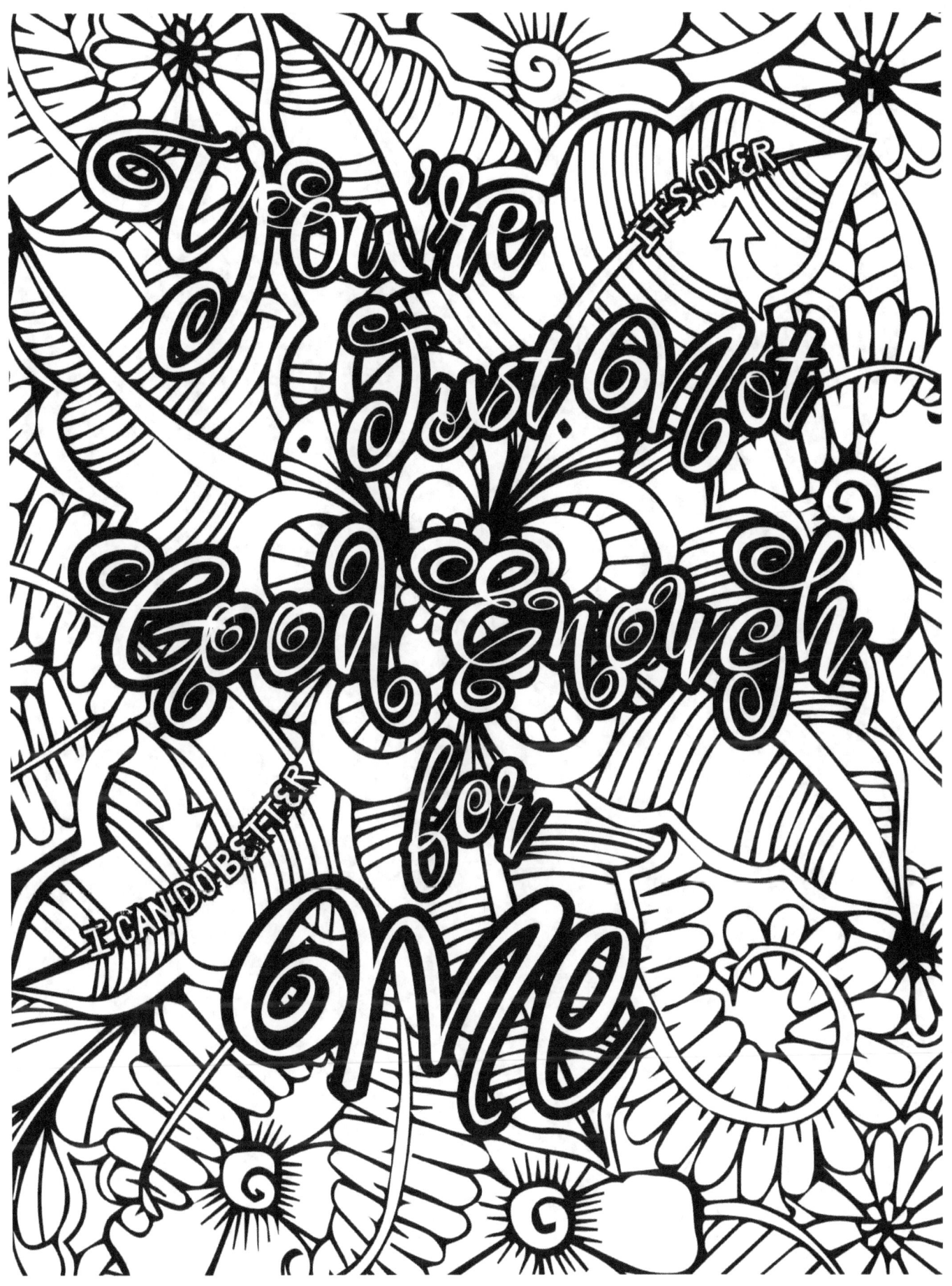

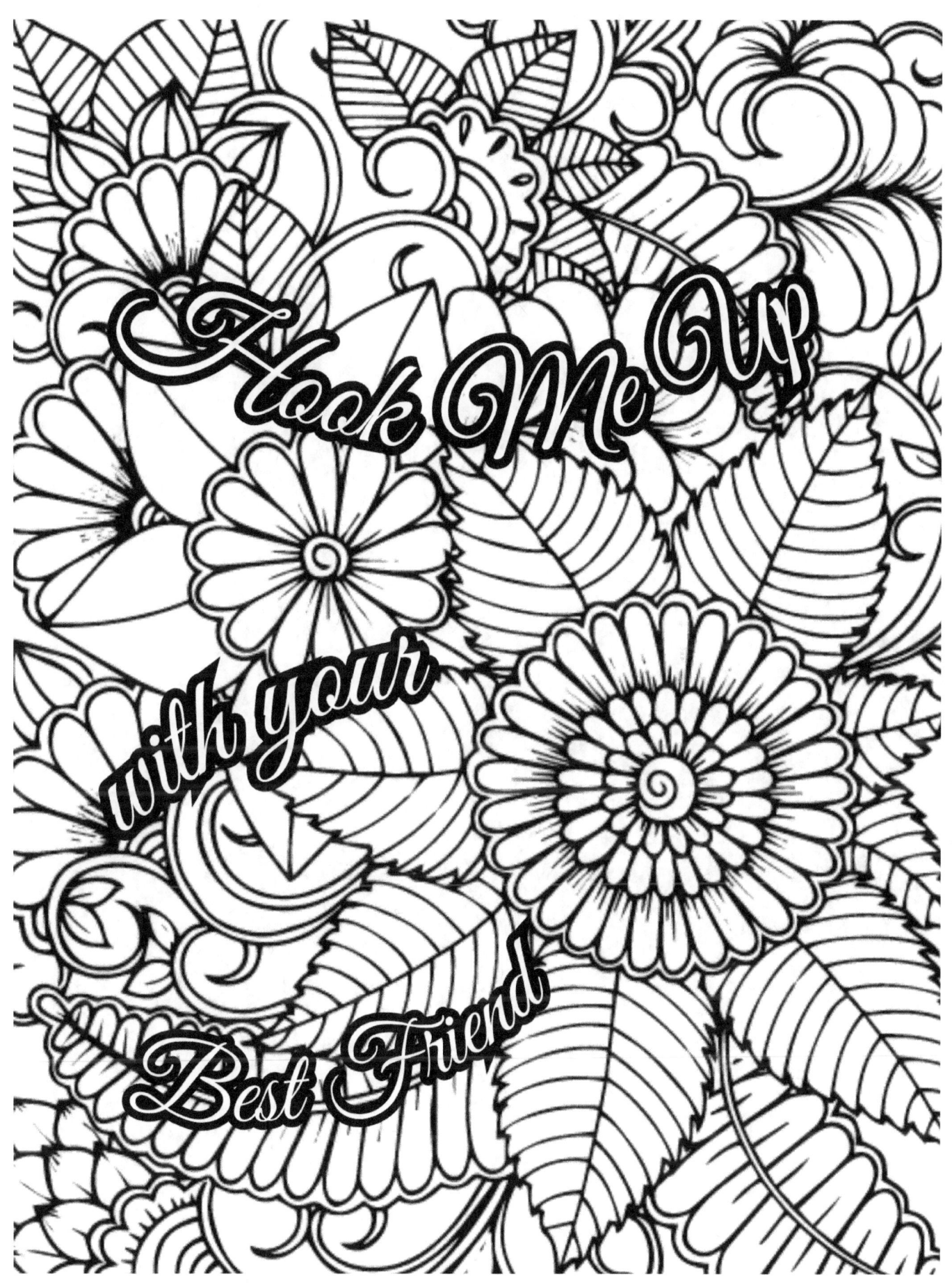

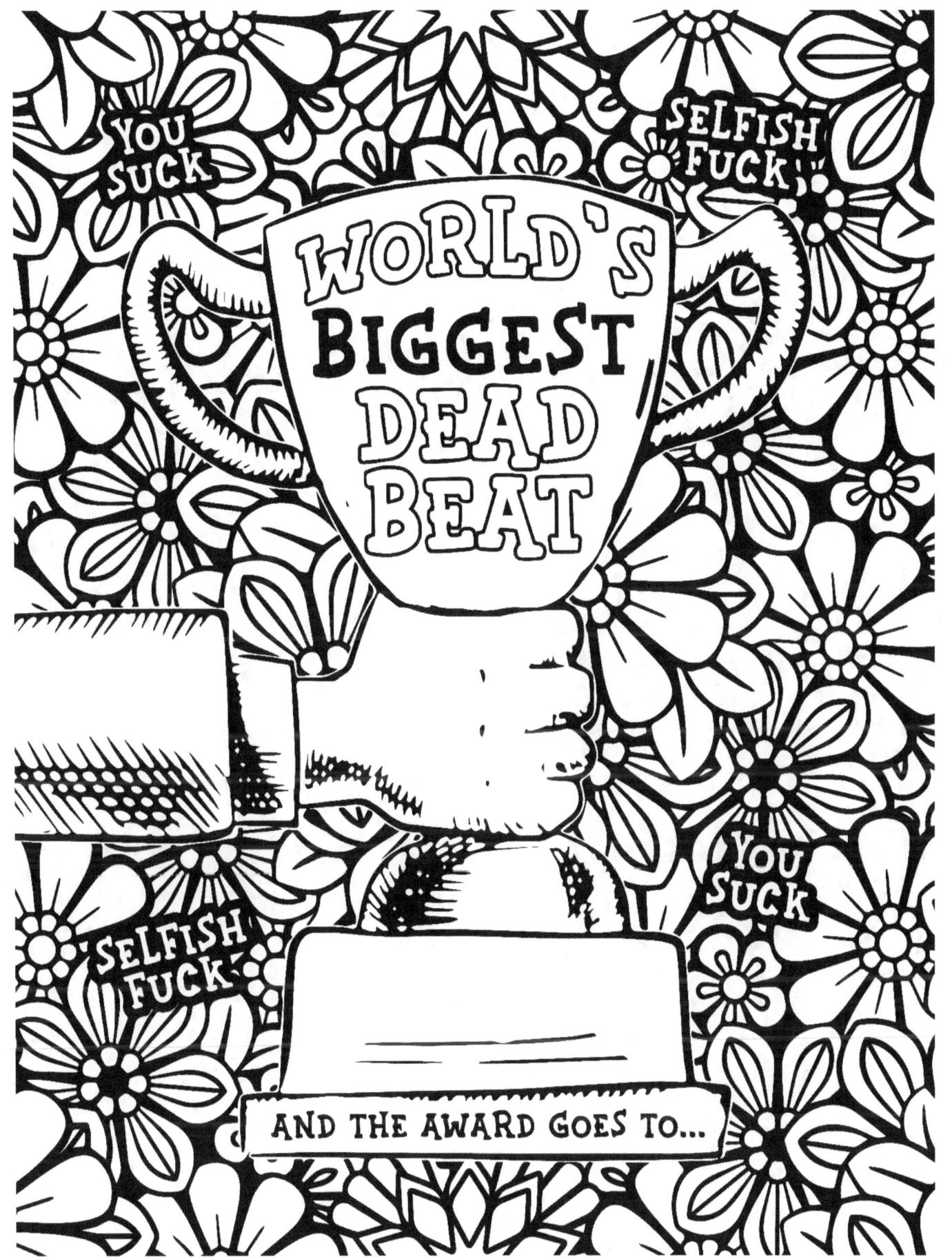

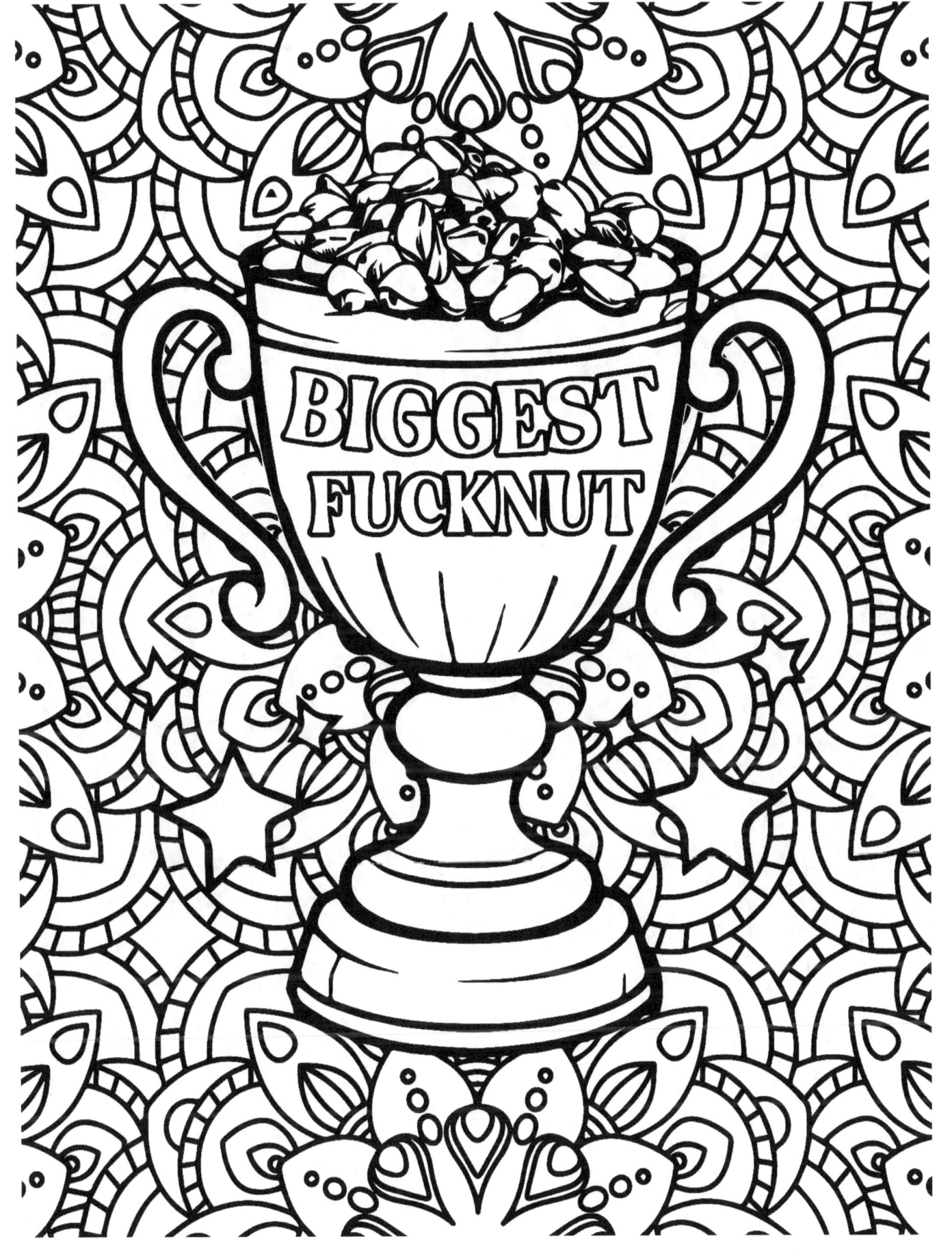

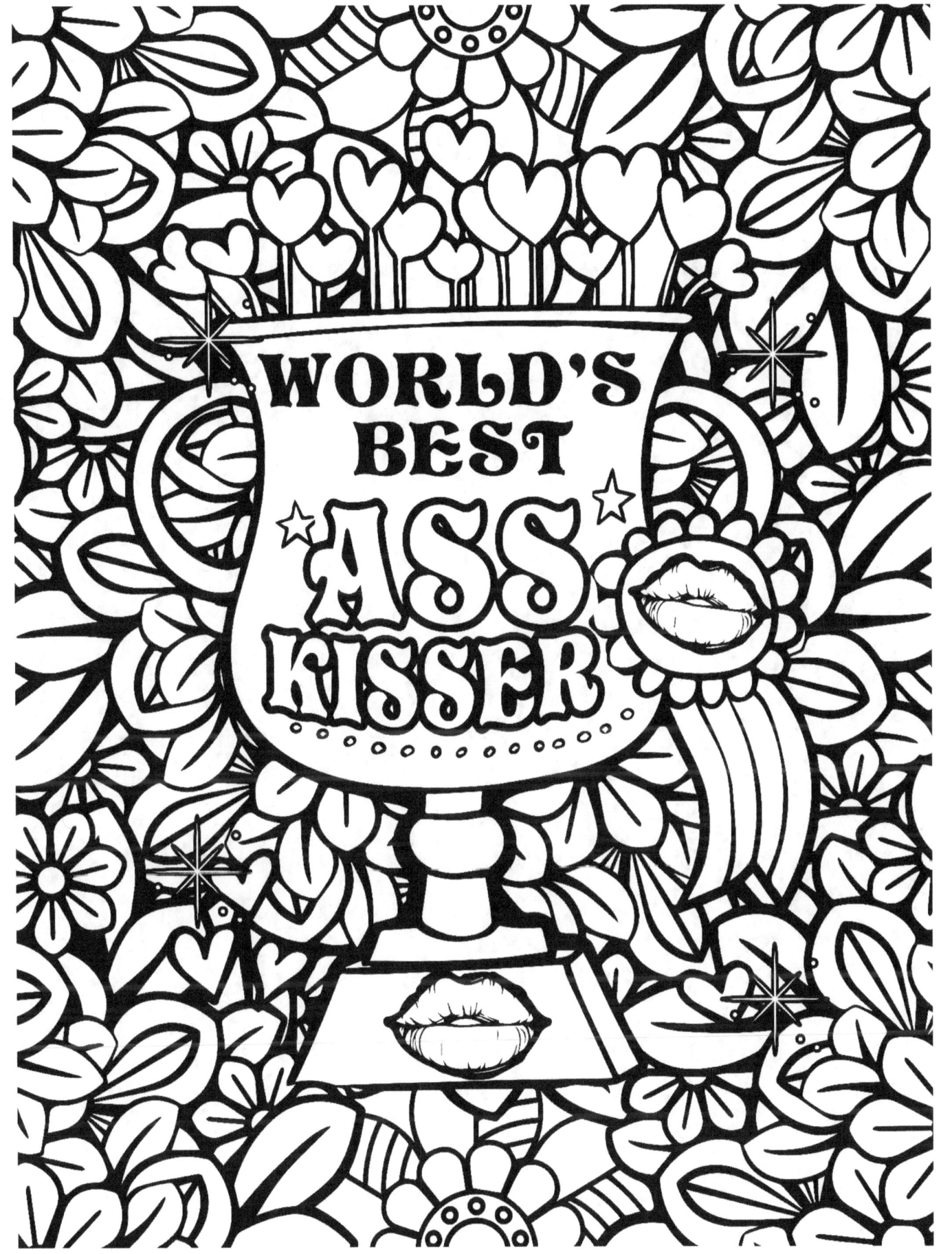

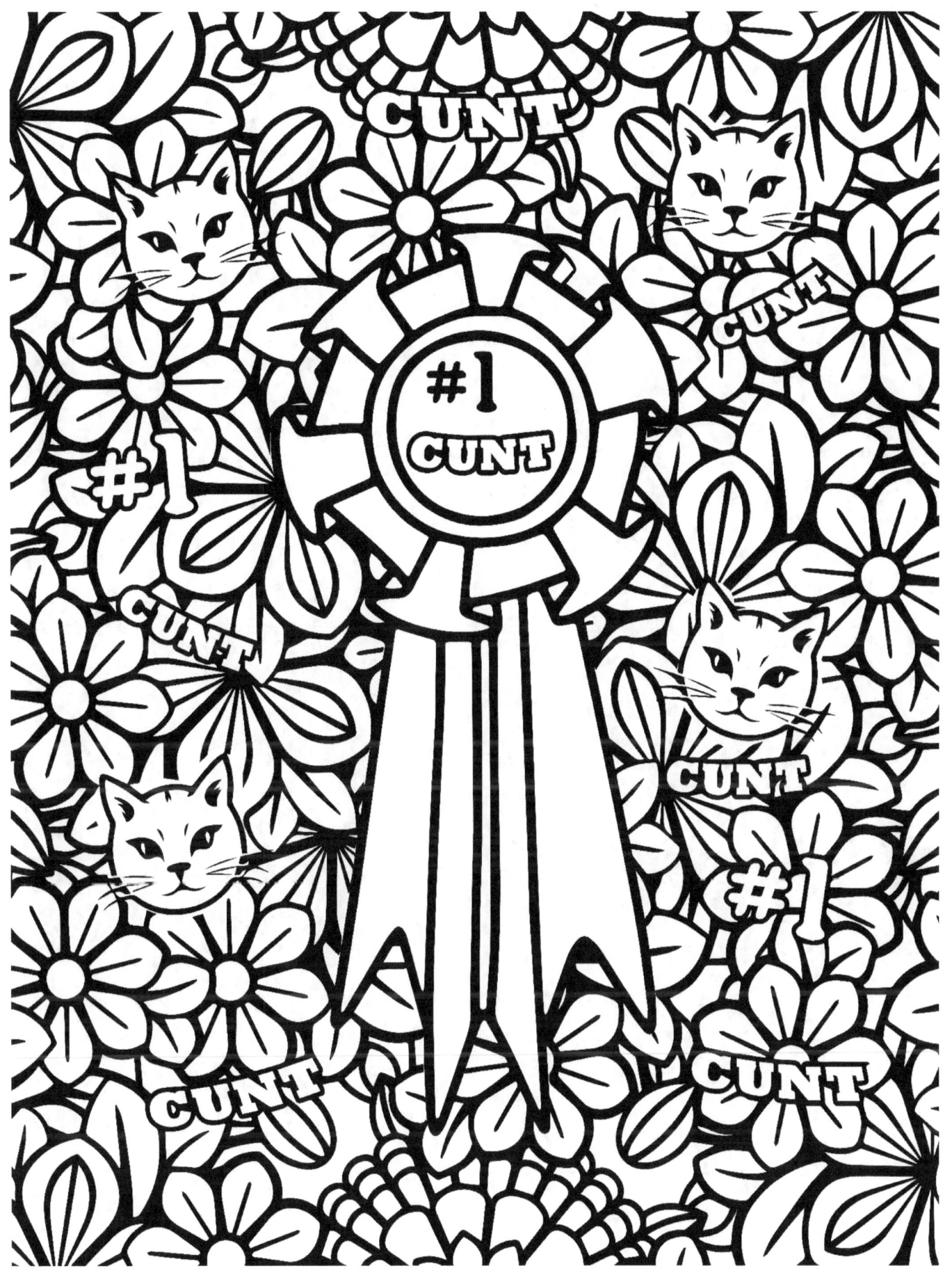

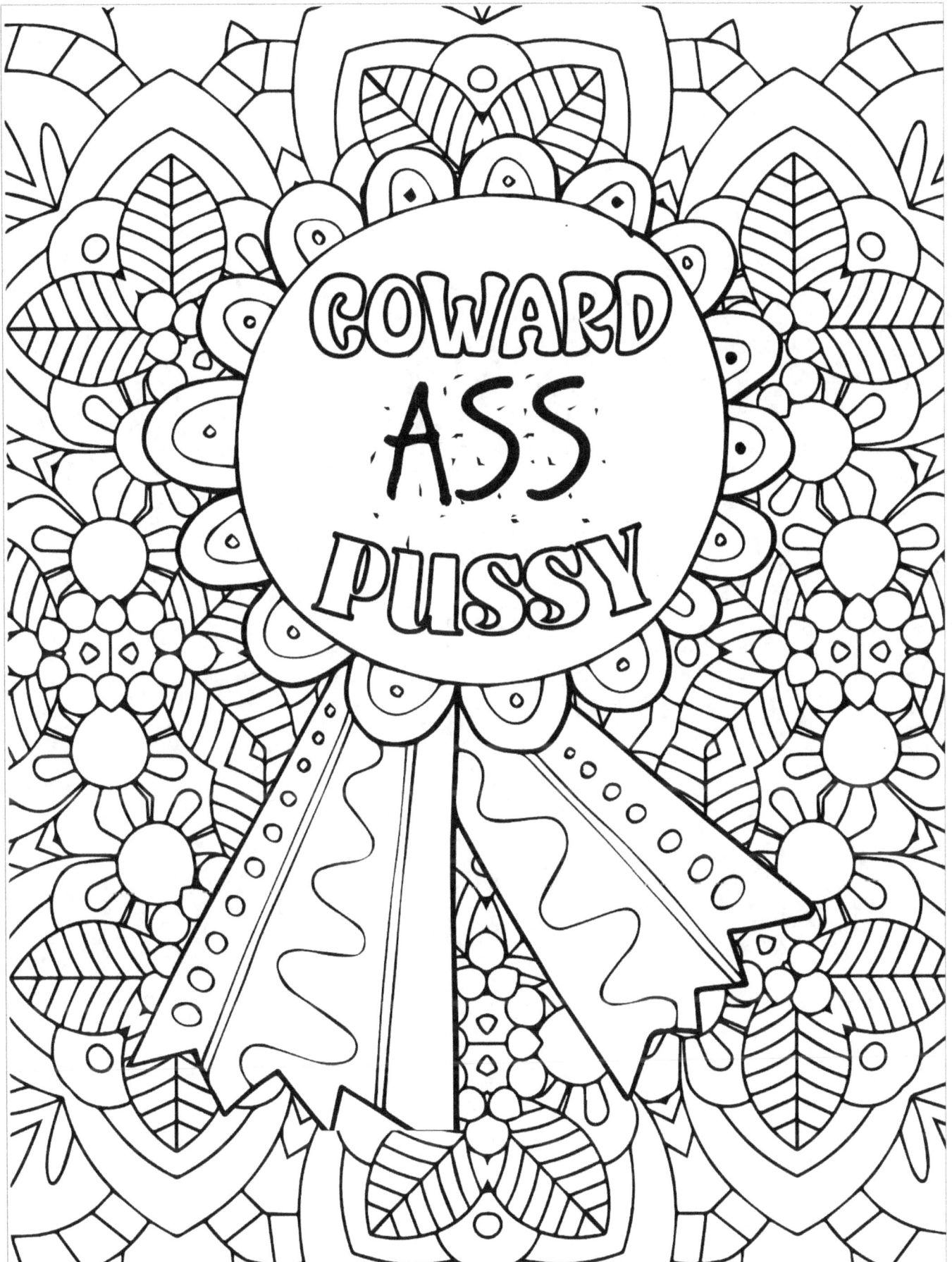

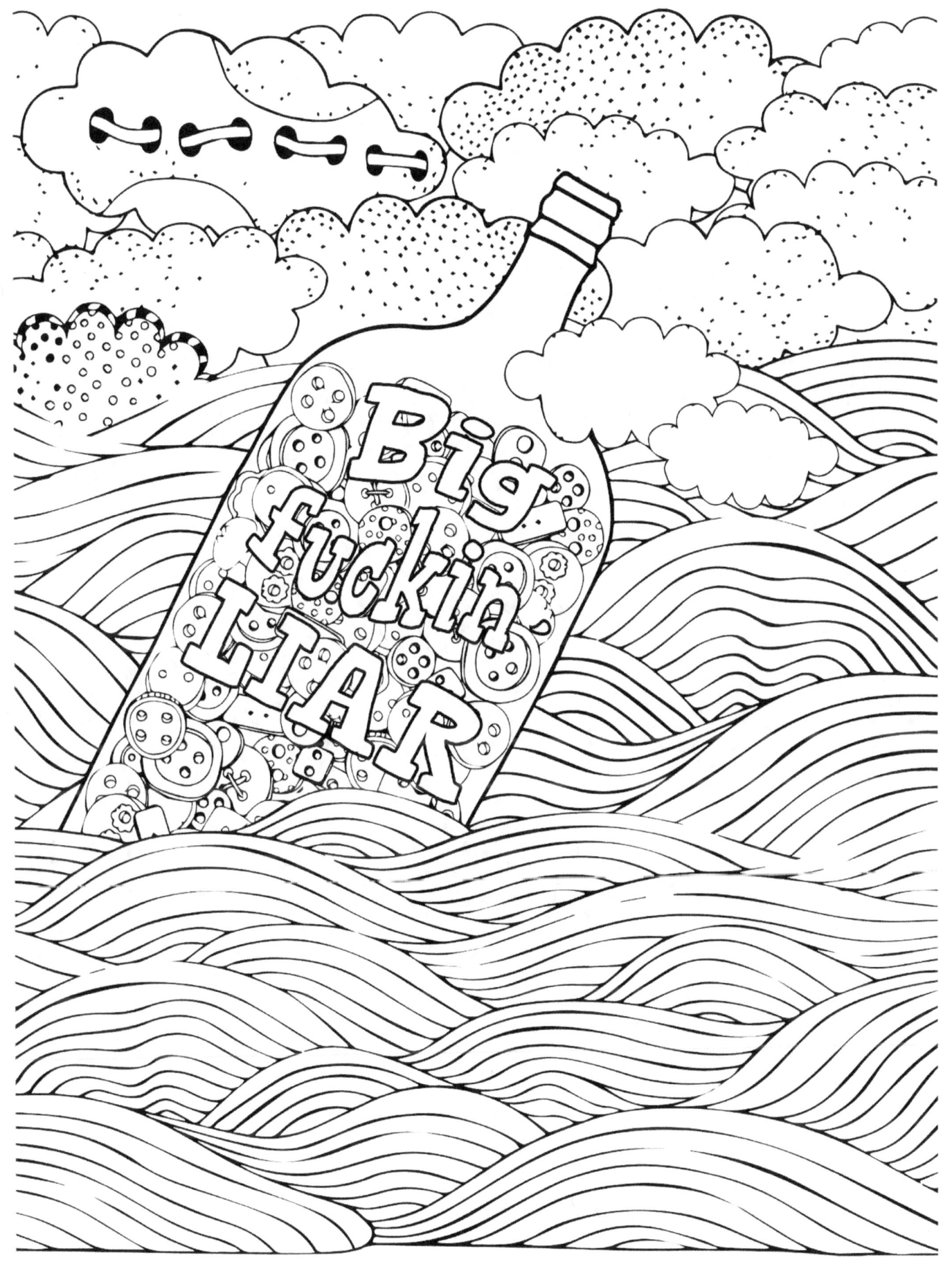

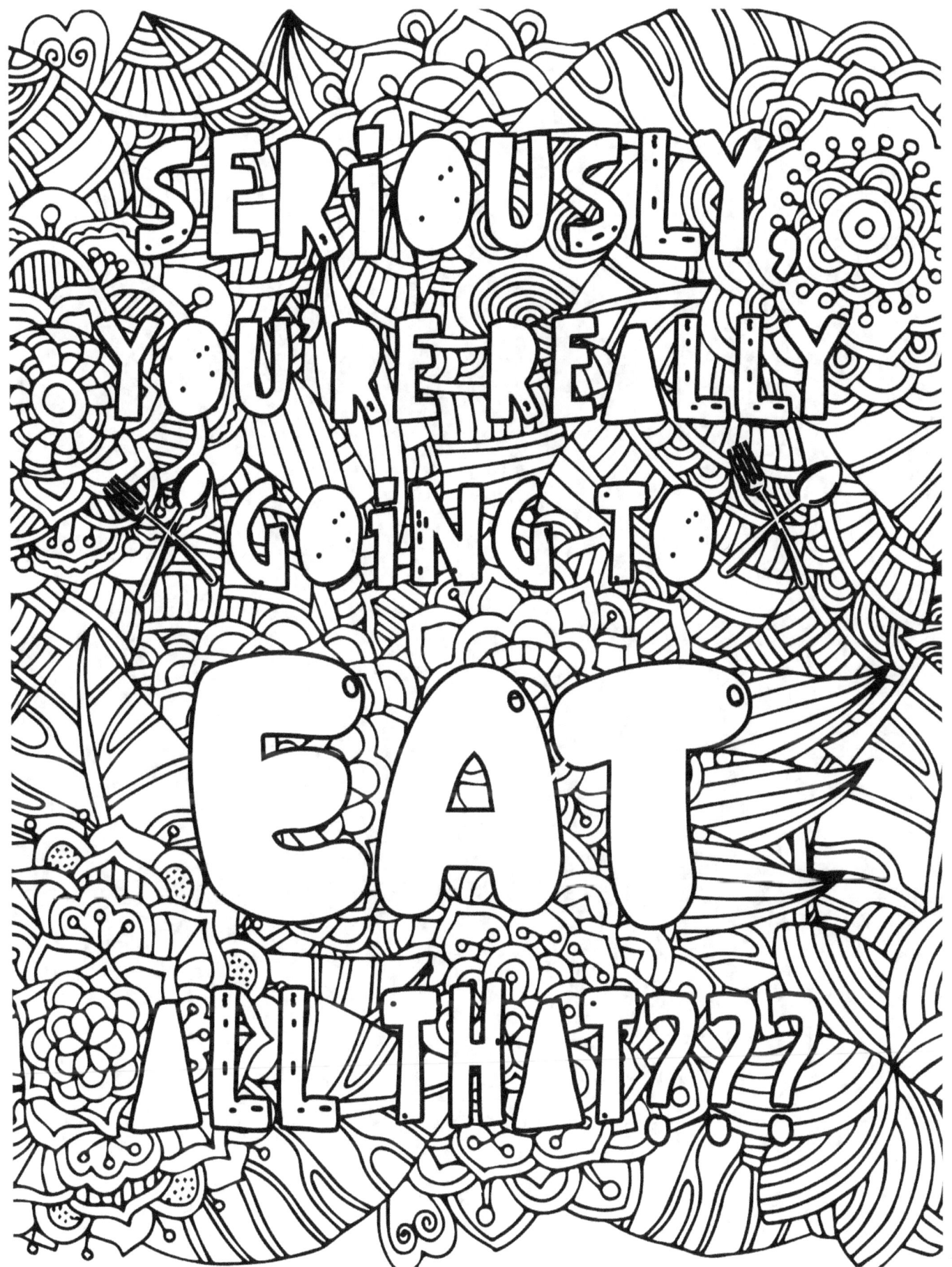

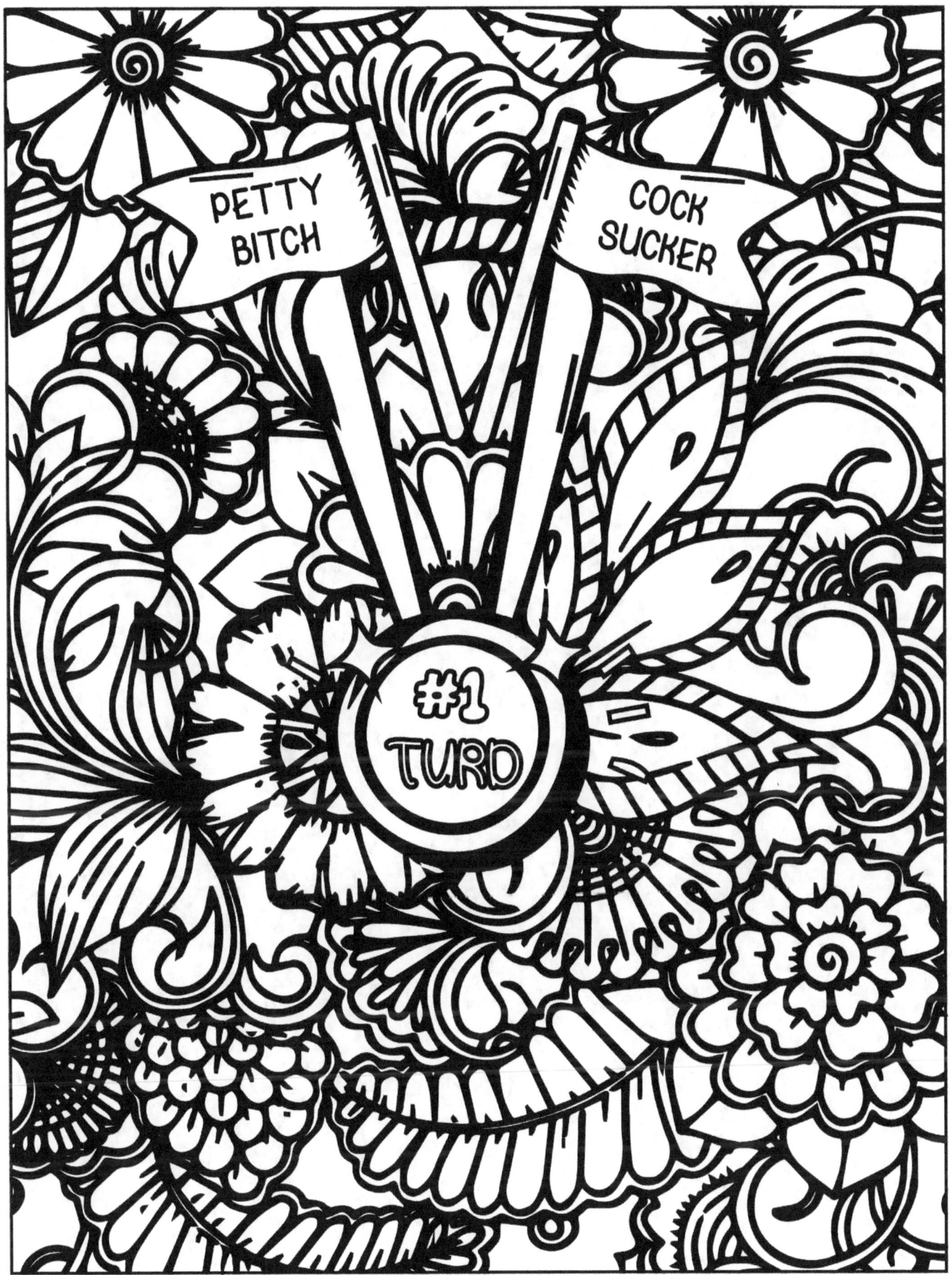

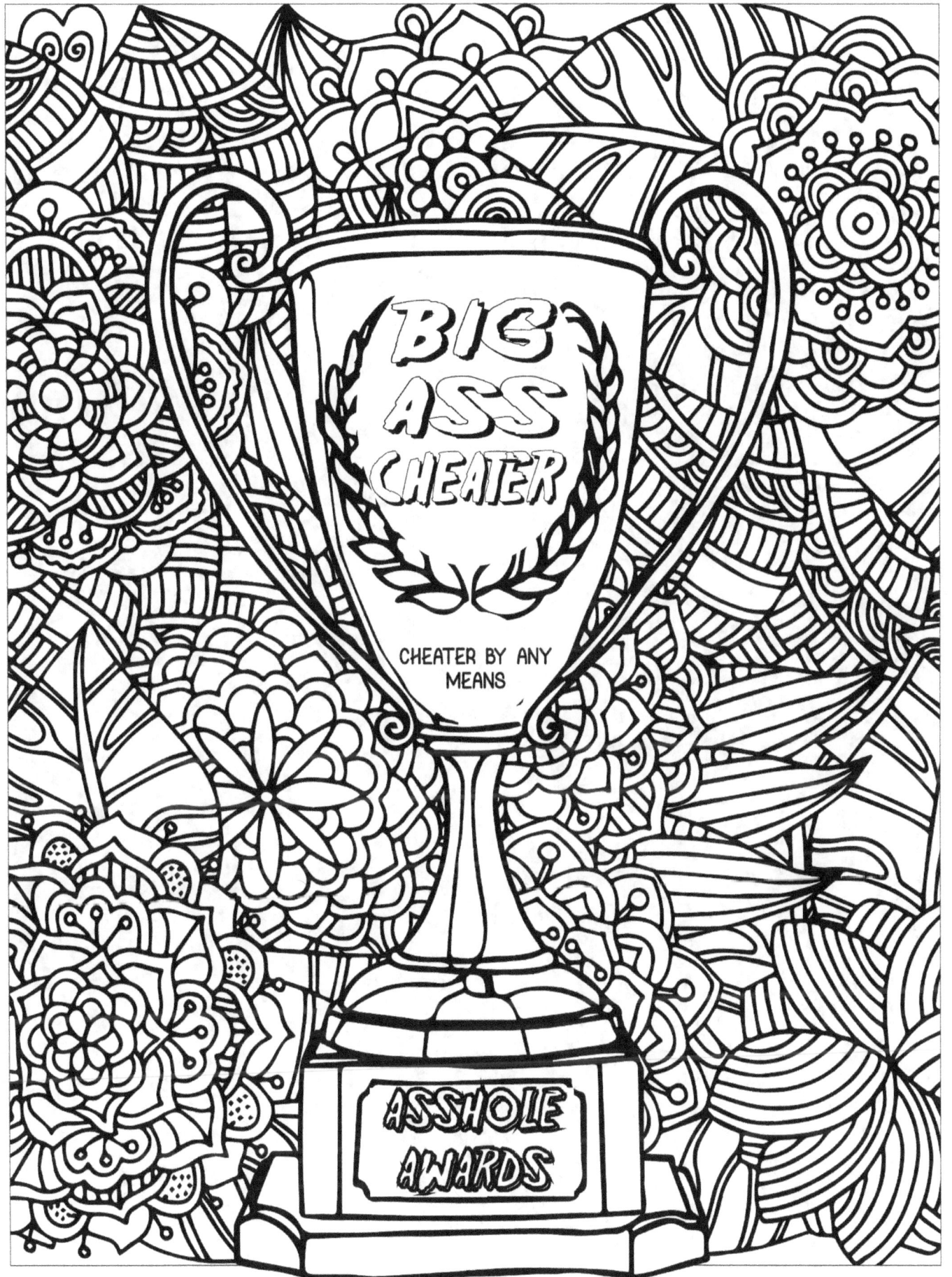

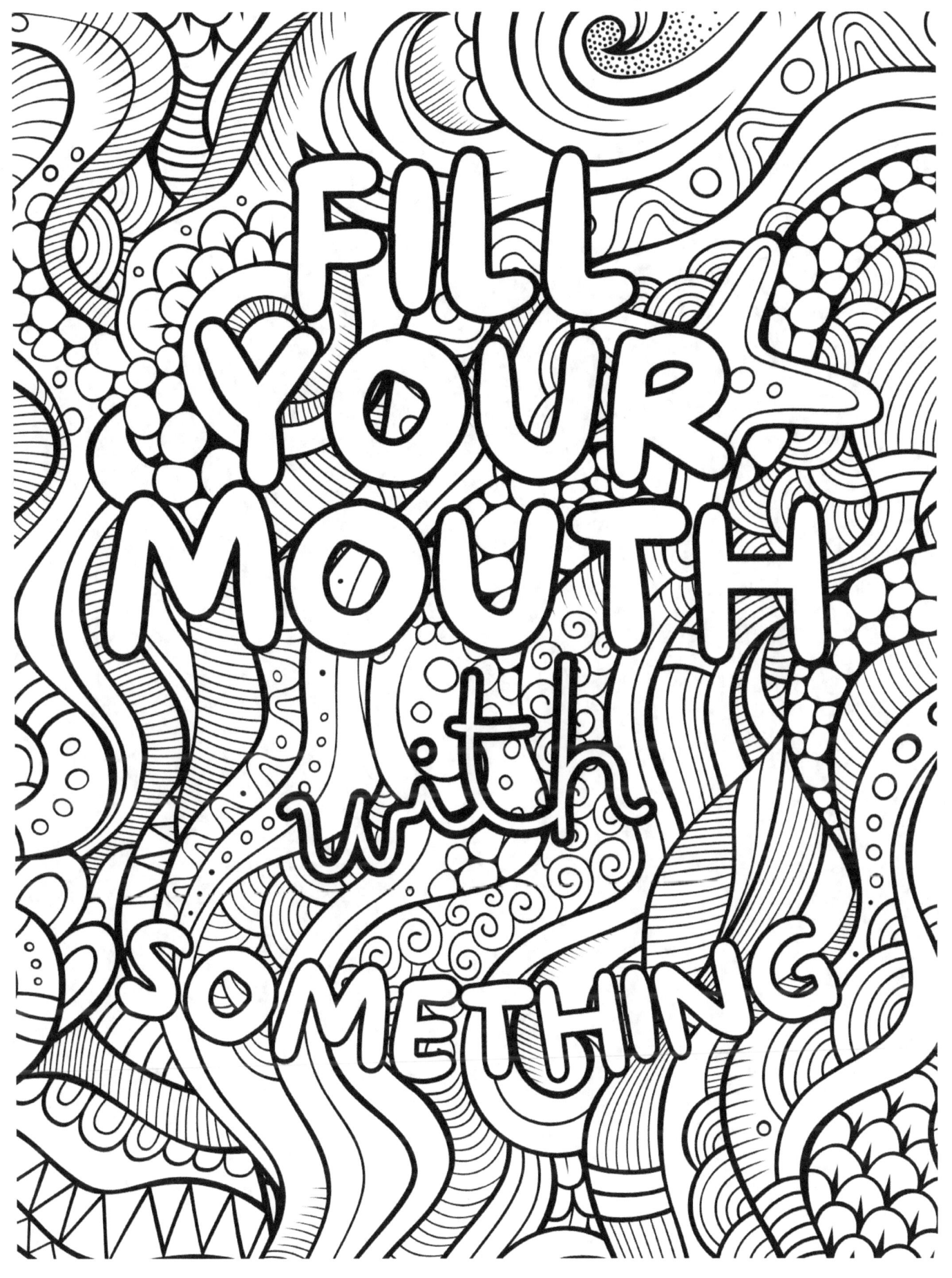

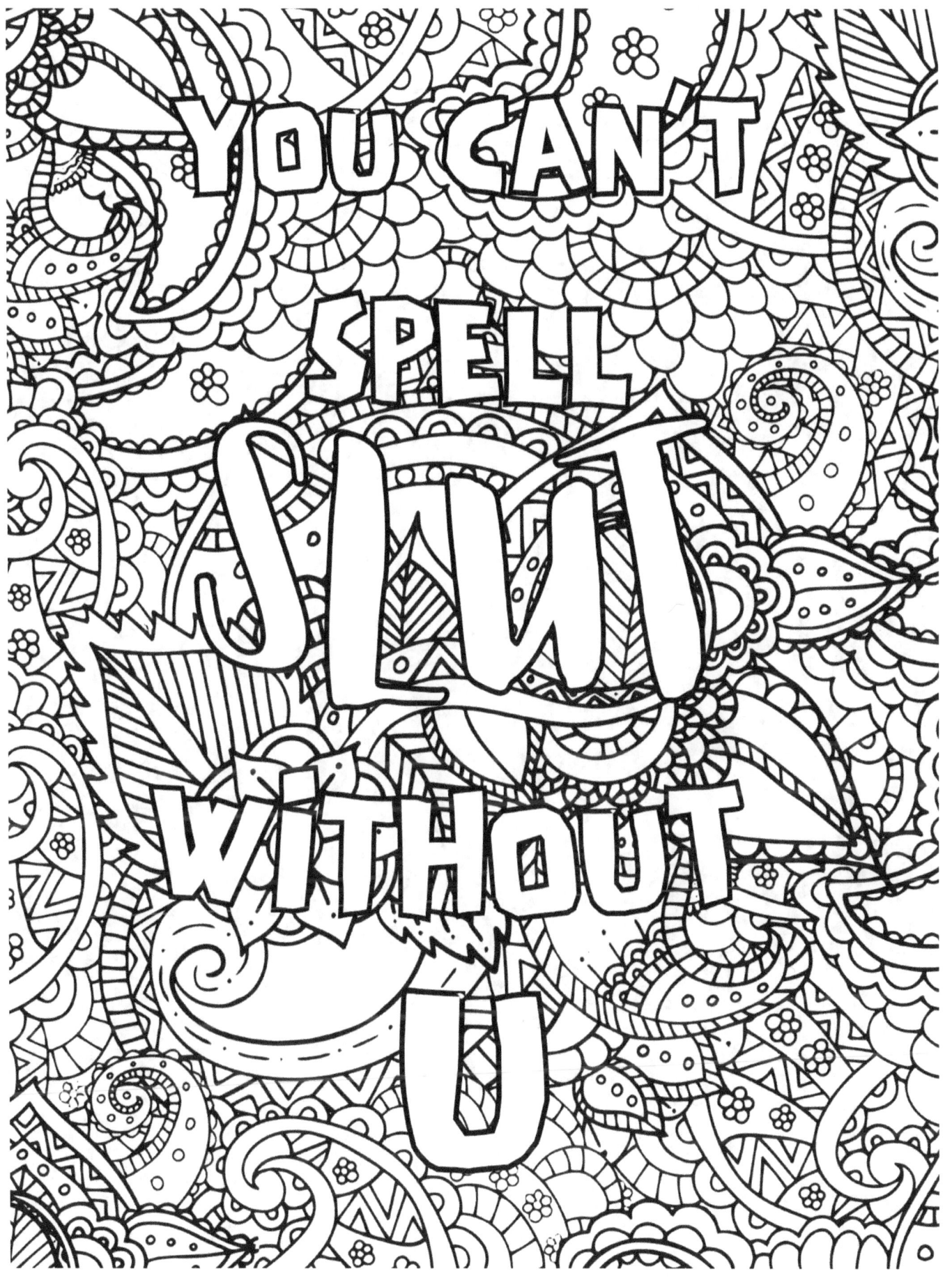

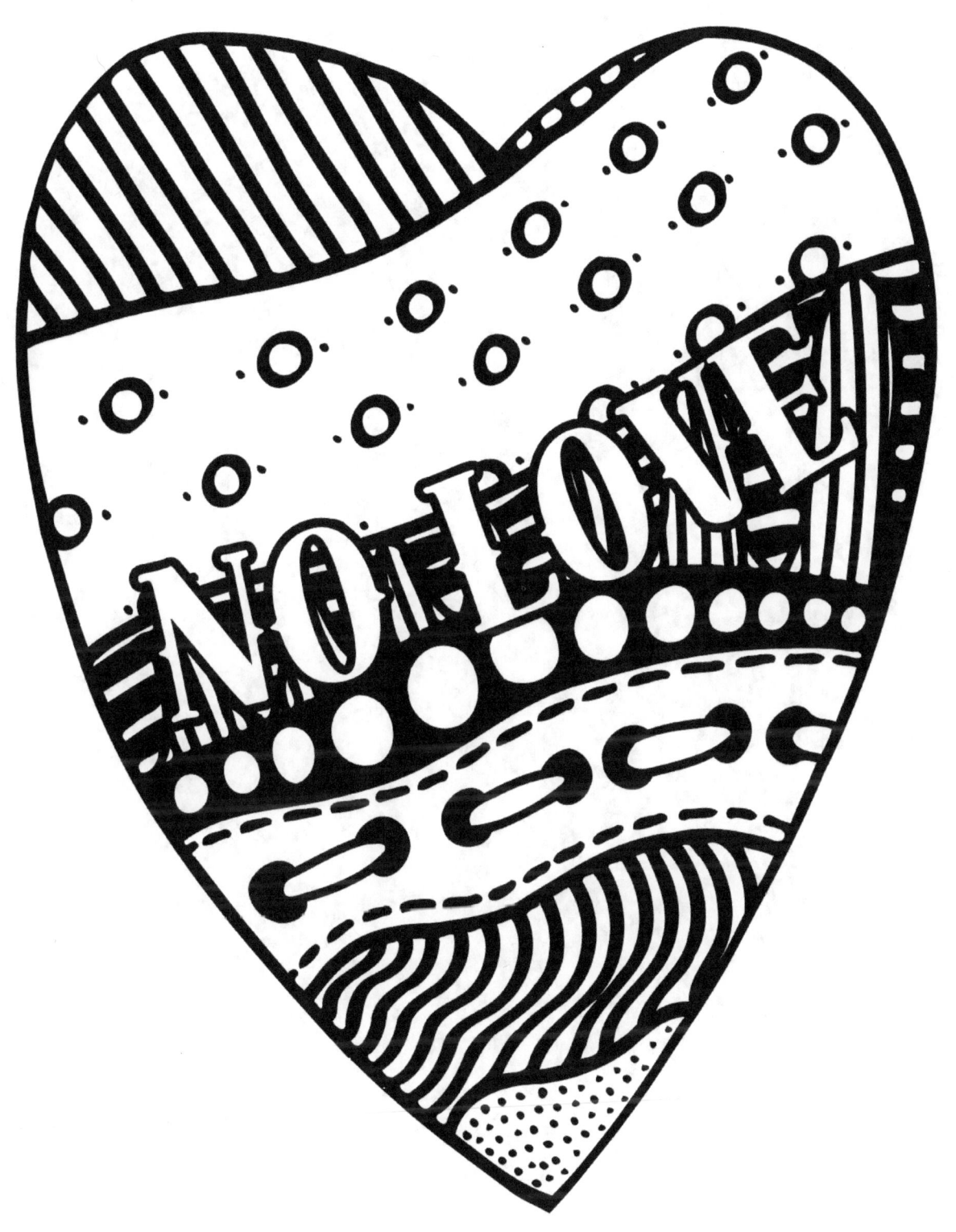